The Z-Series Datsuns

The Z-Series Datsuns

A collector's guide
by Ray Hutton

MOTOR RACING PUBLICATIONS LTD
Unit 6, The Pilton Estate, 46 Pitlake, Croydon CR0 3RY, England

ISBN 0 947981 02 0
First published 1982
Second Edition 1985

Photosetting by Zee Creative Ltd, London SW16
Printed in Great Britain by Netherwood, Dalton & Co Ltd,
Bradley Mills, Huddersfield, West Yorkshire

Contents

Introduction

The automotive world is changing. Japanese cars can no longer be dismissed as uninteresting but well priced and reliable saloons of doubtful styling. There are signs not just of the Japanese catching up with the better products of European industry but, in some areas, taking a technical lead. Their cars are being built in Britain and America. The world's motor industries are coming together.

These days, it is not so easy to point at a car and say 'That's Japanese'. Fifteen years ago there was only one that stood out from the crowd: the Datsun 240Z. It was the most un-Japanese Japanese car. It combined the style of a supercar with the character and performance of an old-fashioned hairy-chested sports car.

The Z was designed for America. It was based on the formula of the traditional British sports cars that had done so well in the USA, but with the important difference of a modern coupe body and such civilized features as wind-up windows and an effective heater. Its E-type looks at a bargain price soon established it as the best-selling sports car of all time. It took the Chevrolet Corvette 25 years to sell half a million; the Z sold 500,000 in less than a decade.

The market that Nissan identified so well when they launched the 240Z in 1969 had changed in those 10 years. The replacement, the 280ZX, followed the same styling theme but was bigger, fatter, heavier and more comfortable — but softer and much less obviously sporting. In turn, its replacement — the 300ZX, launched in 1983 — moved further up-market, combining the 280's comforts with a Turbo V6 engine that provides performance in the Porsche class. Those who own and love the first Z-series are disappointed by the ZX's middle-aged spread, but the sales figures suggest Nissan's strategy was right. In 1984, 300ZX sales in America exceeded the Z's performance in any previous year.

I'll confess more affection for the first series, and in particular the 240Z. Luckily for me, one came with my job as Sports Editor of *Autocar*, and for the 1972 season I used it to cover Grands Prix and other motor sporting events around Europe. At the time it was an almost ideal car for the purpose and it proved 100 per cent reliable. I have driven Zs and ZXs since on both sides of the Atlantic, watched them race, driven and been driven in factory rally cars and followed their progress from the snows of the Monte Carlo Rally to the heat and dust of the Safari.

Nissan didn't just want to sell cars, they wanted to create an image with the Z, one that would establish their reputation throughout the world. So its importance exceeds even its considerable sales. Today, the ZX has similarly sporting rivals from other Japanese manufacturers. When it started in 1969 it was unique. The Datsun Z-cars are the first from Japan to become regarded as modern classics. Hence this *Collector's Guide*. Whether you own one of these cars, or are simply enthusiastic about them, I admire — and share — your taste.

RAY HUTTON

Acknowledgements

At the time of the first edition of this book I was Editor of *Autocar* and, as such, able to call upon that magazine's considerable information and photographic resources. It is appropriate to acknowledge those who produced many of the photographs reproduced here, notably photographers Peter Cramer and Ron Easton. I am also indebted to our close associate, and author of several books in this series, Graham Robson, for his help on the 'Buying a Z-car' chapter.

In addition to *Autocar*, the British magazine *Motor* and the American monthlies *Car and Driver*, *Motor Trend* and *Road & Track* provided a good deal of important test information. The International Division of Nissan Motor Company were most helpful and I thank Hamish Cardno of Nissan UK Ltd not only for filling in the missing links in the Z's British career, but also for acting as liaison with his colleagues in Tokyo and Los Angeles in bringing the international story up-to-date. What's now called the Nissan Motor Corporation in the USA and their long-time PR agency Bob Thomas & Associates patiently sorted out a lot of detail information to build on the story to which they had contributed in 1982.

As then, special thanks are due to some who were particularly involved in the car's development: Albrecht Goertz, Peter Brock, Rauno Aaltonen, Tony Fall and Mike Wood. And to James Morris, press officer of the lively British Z-Club, whose beautifully-restored and very original 1972 240Z I first saw at an informal *concours* when I was invited to talk to the Club and which now appears with Nissan UK's 300ZX Turbo on the dust jacket of this second edition.

R.H.

CHAPTER 1

My Fairlady

Sports car ancestors

In the sports car world one cannot get away from the influence of Great Britain. MG and Jaguar, Austin-Healey and Triumph, set the postwar style for the kind of open two-seater that everyone, from California to New South Wales, recognized as a 'sports car'. It was a legacy of the sporting successes of the 1920s and 1930s. The early postwar years saw a big export drive by the British car makers and a new enthusiasm for their products, especially in the United States. French, German and even Italian car design veered in other, generally more mundane, directions. Detroit, feeling healthy and secure, was building up to a new high in automotive extravagance. They had no need to worry about a few thousand sports car enthusiasts. Fuel crises and 'downsizing' were more than a quarter of a century away. Japan, defeated in war, shattered and underdeveloped, was way across the Pacific. In the car business it could have been on another planet.

For, in the 1950s, the Japanese car industry didn't amount to much. Gradually being reconstructed under American guidance, it had built up to a total production of 13,354 cars in 1955, the year in which many of the factories were returned to their previous owners by the US occupational forces. Many of those cars were foreign designs produced under licence, including some from Britain. Among them were Austin A40 Somersets built by the Nissan Motor Company Ltd in Yokohama, a firm that had been established in 1933 to build the light cars known as Datsuns. These days, when Japanese car exports to Britain exceed 160,000 a year and they sell over 2 million a year in the United States, it is illuminating to recall that from 1946 to 1955 Japan exported just 22 cars. . . .

A little open four-seater of prewar looks, called simply the Datsun Sports and made in very small numbers in 1952, is not, therefore, of any more than curiosity value in the ancestry of the best-selling sports car of all time. Its model code was DC-3 and it shared a 20-hp 860-cc four-cylinder side-valve engine and three-speed gearbox with the contemporary DB-2 baby saloon. Maximum speed was 43 mph.

The British Motor Corporation, as it then was, had a considerable influence on Nissan's design thinking in the 1950s. After the A40 came the A50 Cambridge saloon, and by 1956 Nissan had been able to produce an Austin completely from Japanese-sourced parts. That signalled the beginning of large-scale car production. A new boxy little saloon, the 210, known as the Datsun 1000, was soon to appear, and not far behind was a more genuinely sporting car, the S211. An open four-seater again, it borrowed styling ideas and, in particular, the curved two-tone side panels from the Austin-Healey of the day.

The 1959 S211 used the 210's running gear and 34-bhp 988-cc overhead-valve engine. Though it wasn't exactly a road burner (70 mph maximum) it did show the possibilities of using standard saloon components in a car of quite different character. The S211 had a glass-fibre body, ideal for the small production of this exploratory model, but also somewhat *avant garde* at a time when Lotus and others were pioneering plastic bodywork for European production cars. A few months later the S211 became the SPL212, with the 1,189-cc engine of the first Bluebird 310 saloon. A further version, the SPL213, using an uprated version of the same engine with 55 instead of 48 bhp, completed this series of Datsun 'roadsters'. Only about 500 of these cars were made and they continued to be sold until 1963. But by then

Sports cars for America. The Datsun 1600 Roadster was the first Japanese two-seater to find favour with enthusiasts overseas. This shipment, about to be loaded on to one of Datsun's special car carriers, was bound for the USA, where the majority of these SP311s were sold.

This dumpy little car was called the Datsun Sports and designated DC-3. It shared an 860-cc engine with the 1951-2 DB-2 saloon and was the first 'fun' car (it wouldn't be fair to call it a sports car) to be built in postwar Japan.

something much more exciting — or threatening, depending on your viewpoint — was on offer.

While, if we are being generous, the S211 and its successors bore a rounded resemblance to the Austin-Healey, the first 'proper' Datsun sports car turned out to have affinities to the MGB. The era of export had begun. Nissan had set up a subsidiary company in the United States in September 1960, and with a couple of years of operation through East and West Coast distributors behind them, they were beginning to understand the potential of the American market.

This was the era of the MGA, the TR3A and the Healey 100-Six. Nissan wanted to compete squarely with the British — to offer an open sports car at a reasonable price — and now they had learnt how to do it, using high-volume production components in a different package: the very same formula that produced the British sports cars that the Americans loved. The result was the SP310. They called it the Fairlady.

It was shown for the first time at the Tokyo Motor Show in 1961, but didn't go on sale until a year later. The Fairlady lacked the grace of the MGB, but shared the same square-cut lines and

A bit more like it — Datsun S211 had a glass-fibre body clothing the mechanicals of the 210 saloon. It was made in small numbers in 1959 and led to two further versions with the engine from the first Bluebird.

First proper sports car — the Fairlady 1500 SP310 — was the first of a series of Roadsters, which had styling similarities to the MGB. The 1500 went on sale in 1962 and was a three-seater, with the third occupant sitting across the rear of the car. A year later it was changed to a conventional two-seat configuration.

SP311 took the place of the 1500 in 1965. This is a Japanese domestic-market right-hand-drive car with deep head restraints and a built-in roll-over bar. The Fairlady 1600 continued in production until the arrival of the Z-car at the end of 1969.

even the same kind of scooped headlamp nacelles. It was higher and narrower — the latter to meet Japanese regulations, which levied part of road tax on car width — but it is still tempting to talk of plagarism. Since the MGB was not publicly announced until 1962 it is more likely that both reflected the 'tidy' style of the time. That the Datsun did so represented a great leap forward; for the first time their offering was not an odd, awkward Oriental creation, but something that looked up-to-the-minute and stylish.

The SP310 was unusual in being a three-seater. Two conventional sports car bucket seats were joined by another set cross-ways behind the (right-hand) driver; there wasn't a suitable well for the third passenger's legs and the front seat adjustment was correspondingly limited, so this aspect of the design was not altogether successful.

A steel body clothed a box-section chassis-frame, which tapered towards the front and had cruciform bracing at the centre. A 1,488-cc four-cylinder engine was mounted well forward at the front, driving a four-speed gearbox and a live axle. Front suspension was by wishbones and coil springs, the rear by semi-elliptic leaf springs. Not a very advanced specification, even by

early-1960s standards, it is true — the Fairlady 1500 had drum brakes all round and only 71 bhp in its original form — but it did have unsporting creature comforts like wind-up windows.

By mid-1963 the 1500 had lost its funny third seat and gained 9 more bhp, mainly through the adoption of twin SU-type carburettors. Nearly 7,000 of the SP310 models were made, almost half of which were sold in America.

Our Fairlady became the SP311 in 1965 with a short-stroke 1,595-cc R-series engine delivering a maximum of 90 bhp at 6,000 rpm, an all-synchromesh four-speed gearbox, diaphragm-spring clutch, disc front brakes and other innovations. The Fairlady 1600 was to become the mainstay of the Datsun sports car range through until 1970.

Two years later, in March 1967, it was joined by the SR311, the Fairlady 2000. This put the car into an altogether higher performance bracket. The SP311 1600 had a power-to-weight ratio roughly comparable with a contemporary MGB, which meant that it was fast enough to be fun, but could easily be out-run by less obviously sporting cars. Now, with the specially designed U20 1,982-cc overhead-camshaft four-cylinder engine,

The Fairlady 2000 was a parallel model to the 1600, with the same chassis and bodywork, but an overhead-cam 2-litre engine and a five-speed gearbox. This version has the optional hardtop, which makes it the nearest thing to the Z's direct production ancestor.

The Datsun Roadsters were very popular in club racing in the United States and, even in 1981, this 1600, driven by veteran racer Joe Hauser, could win its category in the SCCA National Championships at Road Atlanta.

the Datsun would have 145 bhp. Also new was an all-syncho five-speed gearbox, and yet initially the 2000 weighed in a few pounds lighter than the 1600. By 1968, the first effects of tightening safety and emissions regulations were beginning to be felt. In its definitive form the 2000 was supposed to be good for 125 mph, but later US export cars with 135 bhp (twin SUs instead of Solex carbs) claimed only 118 and a standing quarter-mile in 17 seconds.

The 2000 Sports, as it was known in America, became the spearhead of Nissan's US competition programme, which was co-ordinated from 1967 by an official Competition Department based in Los Angeles. But although it was easy to make the car fast with the strong new engine, the Fairlady was showing her age and race preparation specialist Peter Brock recalls that it was very difficult to make it go round corners respectably: 'The 2000 had the worst tread (track)-to-wheelbase ratio of any car going. It was very difficult to make a race car with a 47-inch rear track . . .' Nonetheless, the Datsun Sports has proved one of the longest-lived in America's club racing and both 1600 and 2000 models continue to race — and win — in SCCA events.

Some 40,000 SP and SR311s, 1600 and 2000, were made over a period of six years and by the end the two models were identical except for the engine and transmission. Later 1600s had a five-bearing engine and 96 bhp. There was also an optional hardtop in the last couple of years, which proved more popular in Japan and some other markets than it did in the USA.

By 1970 Datsun were well established worldwide; in 1969 their total exports had exceeded 300,000. They had become the world's seventh largest car manufacturer and Japan was challenging Germany for second place in the vehicle production league, behind America. Although Japanese cars had failed to make a major impact in Europe — and motor industry commentators were at a loss to know why, when they had done so well, so quickly, elsewhere — the major firms were fully represented in most European countries. But for most of those markets the Fairlady was not among the models on offer. The 1968 and 1969 Monte Carlo Rally entries of 2000s nominally originated in Finland (Hannu Mikkola drove one) and a few such cars were sold there, but they never came to Britain. In fact, the British importer, Datsun UK Ltd, trod very carefully in the early days

Here it is! The Nissan Fairlady Z as it first appeared in Japan in 1969. This model, for the home market, had a 2-litre six-cylinder engine. Note the rather crude hub caps and the plain Z badges — first export cars had '240Z' on the rear quarters and 'Datsun' on the nose motif.

First glimpse for British enthusiasts was at the Motor Show at Earls Court, in October 1970. Datsun UK described the 240Z as 'every inch a true sports car', but had not at that time decided whether to import it. Only a very few cars were sold in this form, without spoilers and with narrow air-extractor grilles below the rear window.

and were — to some extent, still are — very selective in the cars they offer from Nissan's confusingly large range. When the 240Z was announced in 1969 they were not at all sure that they would sell it, partly because they were not very keen on being in the sports car business, but also because initial demand in America was so high that the factory could not be sure that they could supply them.

Following a now traditional pattern, the Z-car was previewed at the Tokyo Motor Show in November 1969. The first car to appear in Britain was at the 1970 Motor Show at Earls Court,

when Datsun UK put one on their stand to 'gauge reaction'. At about the same time the first rally cars arrived in preparation for their team effort in the RAC Rally. Reaction, both at the show and in the forests, was highly favourable. The first batch for sale arrived the following summer.

In Japan, the new car was the Fairlady Z, so that its lineage was clear, even if the Z was in almost all respects a completely different proposition to its predecessor. Primarily it was a fixed-head coupe, following on from the hardtop roadsters introduced in 1968. Notwithstanding its up-to-date specification, the thing

Datsun origins — this Model 10 dates from 1933, soon after the present name was adopted. The first Datsun car had a 405-cc engine and affinities to the contemporary Austin 7.

that gave it such an instant appeal was its style, the way it looked.

It was designed for America and it is not an exaggeration to say that it was a sensation when it was unveiled there at the end of 1969. A sensation — and a turning point. For instead of following, copying the example set by others, the Z set a trend of its own. A Japanese rather than a British product was to be the pacesetter in the sports car world of the 1970s.

What's in the name

The name Datsun has, literally, arisen from the complexities of the Japanese language. In 1911, an American-trained engineer, Sotaro Hashimoto, founded the Kwaishinsha Company to build the first Japanese motor car. The car was called DAT, after the initials of his three backers, Messrs Den, Aoyama and Takeuchi. When written in Japanese the sound DAT can also mean 'fast rabbit' or 'hare'. Not, perhaps, the most appropriate description for that early car, but it seemed to present a good image. In 1930, they produced a baby car and christened it Datson, using English to suggest 'child of DAT'. Unfortunately, in Japanese, 'son' can also have the meaning 'to lose'. So the name was quickly changed, in 1932, from Datson to Datsun, the suffix 'sun' referring to the national rising-sun symbol and being without danger of confusion.

The use of Japanese characters on name badges was abandoned in favour of roman lettering during the 1930s; surprising, in view of Japan's insularity at that time. Today, badging and switch labelling even of domestic-market cars is in English.

For many years Nissan, the manufacturers, sold vehicles under both Datsun and Nissan model names; the Nissan marque was used mostly on the domestic market. From 1982 a new corporate identity programme called for the use of the company name on their cars worldwide. The transfer from Datsun to Nissan was a gradual process, but from the Z-car standpoint complete at the 1983 introduction of the 300ZX.

CHAPTER 2

Design in dispute

Goertz influence

The man who provided the American influence for the Z-car was a German. The design that was to set the sports car standard of the 1970s had been completed five years before the 1969 introduction and at one stage consigned to the 'dead' file.

Albrecht Goertz was born in Hanover, but lives and works mainly in New York. A US citizen since before the War, he worked with Raymond Loewy in his early days and set up a prolific one-man design consultancy. He is hardly a household name among car designers and to this day only claims credit for five cars. When he first went to Japan, in 1961, he had only done two — the BMW 503 cabriolet and the startlingly beautiful BMW 507 V-8 sports coupe — though he had worked at Porsche during the development of the 911.

That first visit to Japan was pure speculation. 'I didn't know anybody there, but I thought that something was developing,' he recalls. 'I wanted to get a feeling of Japan, so I went there. I met a few people and it was interesting, but nothing to write home about.' But when he came home he wrote a lot of letters, mainly to car companies, offering his services as a consultant designer. He promised to return to Japan two months later. Mazda — who were working with the Italian designers Bertone at the time — expressed some interest, and so did Nissan. A lot of correspondence and conversation followed and, almost a year later, Goertz had an agreement with Nissan.

Big car companies, particularly Japanese ones, are reluctant to acknowledge the involvement of outsiders in the design of their cars. Designs are the combined effort of a team rather than the master plan of one man. Who actually is responsible for ideas is often never revealed; only in 1980 did Pininfarina admit the major part that his company played in the styling of the Datsun 510 Bluebird. This kind of secrecy was to cause problems for Goertz many years later when the Z's successor was introduced.

He worked differently from the Italian styling houses. They drew their designs, made their models and prototypes in Italy, and shipped them to Japan. Often the final results were quite different from their proposals, having been modified by the companies' styling departments. Goertz, who has no staff of his own, went to work with Nissan's design department. A team of designers were assigned to him and executed his ideas; he went to Japan for a couple of weeks every three months.

The first visible product of this arrangement was a tidy fixed-head two-plus-two coupe built on an SP311 chassis. It was launched at the 1964 Tokyo Show as the Nissan Silvia (a model name that survives on a car of similar character today), coded CSP311, and subsequently known as the Datsun Coupe 1600. It had a modern, Italianate appearance, but its configuration was out of tune with the times; that only 550 coupes were made while the Fairlady roadsters sold in thousands illustrates the kind of cars that were currently popular.

Nissan appreciated that the value of Goertz was his knowledge of American taste. They wanted to produce a sports car specifically for the United States, but what *kind* of sports car? That seems to have been left to Goertz to recommend. Market research, as such, had little influence. According to the designer they had a series of round-table discussions. Goertz suggested 'a two-seater — with room'. Brought up with Porsche rather than with the British traditionalists, he thought it should be a fixed-head coupe.

With refreshing candour, he admits they were influenced by existing designs. As the discussions continued, gradually the idea was narrowed down, using then-current cars as examples. Those that best represented their ambitions were the Porsche 911 and the Jaguar E-type. 'It was very unscientific, really,' Goertz remembers. 'We had a definite idea of size and type — we started with "well, how long is a Porsche? How wide is a Jaguar?".'

The loose brief that resulted from these talks was a designer's delight. Similarities between the Z and the E-type or various Ferraris are indeed ideas borrowed from the style-setting sports cars of the time. This work was being carried out in 1963 when the super-streamlined Jaguar was still fresh and a marvel among mass-produced and reasonably priced sports machinery.

The concept can perhaps be summed up as the style of an E-type, the size of a Porsche. When he had worked for the German firm, Goertz had been opposed to the idea of a 2+2, preferring to give more space for two occupants to ride in comfort. He was determined that the Z should have room for Americans who were usually 6 ft-plus rather than just over 5 ft, like the average Japanese. This required some new thinking at

Albrecht Goertz — a German with a special knowledge of, and feeling for, American taste. He went to the emerging Japanese motor industry with his design ideas.

The car that made the Goertz reputation — the 1955 BMW 507. A model that was made in very small numbers, it nonetheless received universal praise for its clean, lithe, sporting style. It was only the second car that he had designed.

Datsun's first sports coupe — the Coupe 1600 — was better known as the Nissan Silvia and coded CSP311. Goertz produced this, working with a design team in Japan, and it was the first time the company had used clay model mockups in producing a body, a technique that is universal today.

The rear of the Silvia was particularly neat and adaptations of the style kept recurring in Nissan's long-drawn-out development of the final Z-car.

Outside influences. Goertz admits that the Z owes its configuration to the Jaguar E-type coupe (above) and the Porsche 911 (below): 'The style of the Jaguar, the size of the Porsche'.

planned to use wire wheels and originally the design incorporated pop-up headlamps, but the mechanics of such things were thought to be too complicated and so the cut-out 'sugar scoops' in the front wings took their place. He could see no need for racing-style plastic headlamp covers like those of the original E-type.

Though he was a consultant to Nissan, the prototype work for the new car was being carried out by Yamaha with whom they had an agreement. The car was intended to have a new 2-litre twin-cam engine designed by Yamaha, but the engine proved troublesome and when presentation day came and Nissan management were to appraise the prototype it was clear that a number of technical problems remained. They withdrew from the project.

It was not revived until 1966, after Goertz had left. By then, Datsun's arch-rivals, Toyota, had come out with a car that looked, and was, Japan's answer to the E-type Jaguar. The Toyota 2000GT was later to be held as one of the design influences of the

Nissan. The fifth-scale models they used to check interior dimensions were scaled down from 5 ft 4 in. Goertz called for some new figures to be made that represented 6 ft 3 in. . . . Most of the stylists and modellers Nissan assigned to him at that time could not drive (the huge expansion of the car population in Japan was only just starting) and so they had little appreciation of driving positions and the juxtaposition of controls. Goertz does not claim credit for the detail of the Z's American-style interior, only his insistence that the seats should be big enough and that there should be generous space for their bigger clients across the Pacific.

The design was completed towards the end of 1964. Goertz had

The hallmarks of Goertz — the car's stance and the closely-cut wheelarches — are apparent in this early model for the prototype Z that was being built at Yamaha.

Next stage — wooden framework for the full-sized clay model and the prototype that resulted. It has the wire wheels and retractable headlamps that Goertz had planned and is the same in most important areas to the first 1963 model (see page 20) but Goertz says that it was completed by Nissan after the split with Yamaha and he had left.

The '2000GT' prototype alongside an SP311 hardtop — clearly, the final car, even though it would not appear for another four years, would have a more dramatic style than the narrow, conventional, Fairlady Sports.

Z-car. Here was a sleek hatchback two-seater with a 2-litre twin-cam six-cylinder engine, five-speed gearbox and independent suspension all round that coincided with Nissan's aborted plans. And well it might, for after the Nissan project had been abandoned, Yamaha are understood to have taken the idea of such a car with their new engine to Toyota . . . Goertz confines himself to the observation that the Z body and the 2000GT 'could be brothers', and it is noteworthy that the Toyota has wire wheels and pop-up headlamps. . . .

If it was Toyota's intention to beat their competitors to the marketplace with the same type of car, it didn't turn out that way. Though widely praised at its introduction, the Toyota was highly priced and only 1,000 were made. A one-off open version featured in the James Bond film *You Only Live Twice* with the usual range of 007 gimmicks, and the model Twiggy bought the only one to come to Britain, but eventually the 2000GT just faded away.

When they went back to it, Nissan did a lot of rethinking about the Z. They made an unusually large number of full-size clay models, many of which showed open cars, some reminiscent of the Triumph TR6, others Maserati-like. Earlier ideas extending

Another line of approach taken under the direction of Goertz was this open model, known as the SP410. Though it has no direct resemblance to the final Z, it was this design that was gradually modified to give the final coupe style, borrowing ideas from the 'GT' along the way.

the square-cut coupe lines of the Silvia were revived, but they kept coming back to Goertz's concept car. By late-1967, the shape as we now know it was more or less finalized. The screen and windows were shallower, the rear door changed a bit, there was slightly more bodywork below the bumper line than on the prototype, and Goertz's original Corvette-type pointed nose was less pronounced, but the basics were there.

Ideas of convertible versions were rejected, though a longer-wheelbase two-plus-two version was styled in 1968 for later introduction. Goertz didn't believe in either, but by that time had long since ceased to be involved.

He is pleased that the Z turned out as close to his designs as it did. 'It has a certain character,' he explains carefully. 'All my cars lean forwards (a reference to the way in which the air intake slopes backwards) and they have a very tight body/wheel relationship

(the wheels are close to the outer extremities and the tyre treads partly exposed as the wings cut away behind them). They maintained these things and the basic window shapes.'

It is because this 'tightness' of line, like the nose inclination and the relationship of the track to the body width, has changed that Goertz is critical of the 280ZX. He said so to *Car and Driver* in 1979 and his comments brought a statement from Nissan US, published in the American motor industry journal *Automotive News*, denying that Goertz had a part in designing the first Z-car. 'It is absolutely unthinkable that he had a hand in designing the 240Z,' wrote Nissan Motor Corporation Executive Vice-President Hiroshi Takahashi.

Though Goertz can be outspoken, he also has a certain modesty. He was offended. Though reluctant to do so — 'It's ridiculous for an individual to sue a company of that size' — he decided to take legal action to protect his reputation. The matter was settled out of court at the end of 1980 when Nissan sent him a

The Nissan-Yamaha prototype as it was left when Nissan pulled out — a neat, Italian-looking design that was in tune with the GT style of the early-1960s. Note that it did not have a hatchback.

What the Yamaha project grew into — the 2000GT from Nissan's dreaded rivals, Toyota. The style is considerably different in detail from the prototypes, but the important lines and the cars' concept are the same. Compare the three-quarter rear view with 240Z's elsewhere in this book.

letter that clarified the situation. It reads:

'We have examined the relevant evidence pertaining to the development of the highly successful Datsun 240Z which was first introduced in 1969.

'You were retained by Nissan during the period from 1963-65 as an automotive design consultant. During that period you consulted with Nissan on the basic methods of styling a general sports car. You were also the sole design consultant on a 2-litre sports car which Nissan was trying to develop as part of a joint venture with Yamaha. This car was not introduced.

'While it is our view that the design of the 240Z was the product of Nissan's design staff, Nissan agree that the personnel who designed that automobile were influenced by your fine work for Nissan and had the benefit of your designs.'

Or, as Goertz puts it, 'They designed the car, but I showed them how'. He is satisfied by Nissan's public explanation, for as he says, 'What is design? Design doesn't mean a thing. The important thing is the concept. Not whether this guy or that guy did that bolt or that detail.'

Clearly, the Z-car was Goertz's concept, and that is all he seeks credit for. 'Basically, it's a dull car,' he says. 'There's nothing spectacular about it, but things do fit together well. It's harmonious, well balanced, looks finished. Nothing very scientific — it's mostly luck. . . .'

Despite his misgivings about the way it turned out, Goertz is happy not to have been involved in the ZX. 'It is tough to follow a successful car, no matter who did it. It was easy for me with the original car as there were no comparisons.' He hasn't designed a production car since. Talking to the author in 1981, he had just returned from a visit to Japan, but at the age of 67 didn't think it likely that he would be embarking on a new car project. After a design career that has covered everything from cameras and television sets to office and kitchen furniture, he was busy in a completely new field of design — sports clothing.

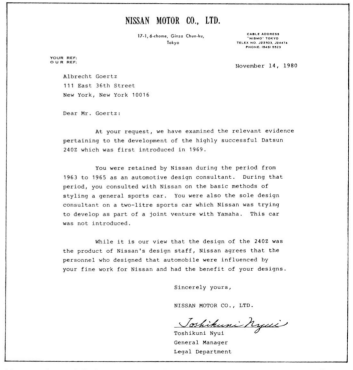

The final solution. Long after Goertz had gone, Nissan adopted the broad lines of his idea for the first Z-cars. His designs had been complete in 1964; the Fairlady Z was first shown to the world at the end of 1969.

Honour is satisfied — the 'settlement' letter from Nissan to Goertz confirming his role as sole design consultant on the Nissan-Yamaha project and his influence on the company's design staff.

CHAPTER 3

Best-selling sports car

The Z arrives

With export to America the prime reason for the new sports car, one might think that the Nissan Motor Corporation in the USA would have provided some guidelines for the Z's design. This was not so, at least in any formal sense. 'In those days we didn't know what we were getting until they came off the boat,' says one long-time employee.

But the President of Nissan US, Yutaka Katayama, did have considerable influence at the head office in Tokyo. Katayama was a former advertising and sales promotion executive and a racing enthusiast. He had founded the Sports Car Club of Japan and, as chief of Nissan's operation in California, was responsible for the Datsun US racing programme that started in the late-1960s. By that time, Nissan were very export-orientated and it is interesting to note that the first President of Nissan Motor Corporation when it was founded in 1960 was Takashi Ishihara, who had been Export Director and, by 1981, was President of the Nissan Motor Company worldwide.

In resurrecting the Z-car project from the Nissan/Yamaha 2000GT, they judged that in the 1970s buyers would want a different kind of sports car. Something that looked exciting and different, that had good performance and taut handling, but that was more comfortable and practical than traditional two-seaters. A GT car like a Porsche or a Jaguar E-type, perhaps not with quite their quality or all-round performance, but at a much lower price. Those more exotic GTs were expensive (yes, 6,000 dollars was dear in 1969!) while in the lower-price bracket there was the choice of coupes that were really thinly disguised saloons or the old-style sports cars in different clothes, like the MGB GT and Triumph GT6. There was room for a lower-priced, high-styled

gutsy enthusiast car that would appeal to the sports car purist as well as the uncommitted car-buying 'single'.

A coupe rather than an open car would, it was thought, have the widest appeal. There were also some 'safety' considerations, reflecting proposals for US legislation that looked as if it would outlaw open cars (uncertainty about this was to influence the design of a number of cars, including the Triumph TR7 and the Jaguar XJ-S, and the matter was not clarified until some years later).

Price would be a key factor. The original plan was for a low-volume production, but if the price was to be right the car had to share major components with other popular models and be made in economically large quantities. A production target of 2,000 units a month was fixed — still small by today's Japanese standards — and the price was to be within a couple of hundred dollars of the MGB GT — around 3,500 dollars by late-1969 values.

Value-for-money became the Z's main sales pitch. There were better cars of the same kind, of course, but none that offered what the Datsun did for the price. For an initial US retail price of 3,526 dollars, no-one else could offer a beefy, overhead-camshaft six-cylinder engine, independent suspension all round, and a body that at a glance could be mistaken for an E-type. The 240Z promised the performance of a Porsche for the price of an MGB GT. (MG enthusiasts, whether later converted to Datsuns or not, may care to note that the MGC GT, which offered a somewhat similar specification, ceased production a few weeks before the Z was announced. It had not been well received, being front-heavy and lacking in typical MG response, but it is tempting to

The American dream — this US publicity photograph of the first 240Z shows that left-hand-drive versions were virtually the same as Zs for other markets in 1970, the only distinguishing features being the badging, rear indicator repeaters and front bumper overriders. The blurb describes the 240Z as a '3500 dollar personalized coupe'.

The 510 Bluebird had blazed a trail for Datsun's overhead-camshaft engines and gained a quick acceptance among American enthusiasts as a car with good performance and tuning potential at a reasonable price. The same basic engine with two more cylinders added formed the heart of the Z-car.

conclude that the Datsun scored in its fresh looks, while the MG was an old design.)

The Datsun range was sufficiently well developed by 1969 to provide the right raw materials for the sports car 'cocktail'. The 510 Bluebird had been introduced in 1967 with a new 1,595-cc overhead-camshaft engine and there were logical production and servicing reasons to stretch this unit from four to six cylinders and use many of the same parts. So the 2,393-cc L24 engine of the 240Z shared the 510's oversquare dimensions, its pistons, connecting rods, bearings and valve gear. Like the four-cylinder, it was a conventional single-overhead-cam engine, with cast-iron block and aluminium head. The camshaft was chain-driven and the crankshaft ran in seven main bearings.

The L24 engine has a remarkable similarity to the 1960s Mercedes ohc six, the design of which was at one time licensed to Prince Motors, who merged with Nissan in 1966 and were renowned for their engine work. It is worth pointing out at this stage, since the variety of Nissan engines — like their models — has always been confusing, that the 510's L16 four-cylinder isn't related to the pushrod R-type used in the Fairlady 1600 (despite

having the same capacity), nor to the U20 ohc engine of the 2000, nor to a couple of other six-cylinder engines around 2-litres offered by Nissan at that time! The L24 did, however, form the basic six-cylinder engine later used in the big Datsun saloons and estate cars.

The standard four-speed gearbox was similar to that of the 510, with different ratios and strengthened for the six-cylinder's extra torque, while the optional five-speed was as offered in the 2000 Sports. The front suspension, using MacPherson struts and simple lower links plus torque arms, was shared with the Laurel 1800 saloon. The rear suspension was unique to the Z, but used MacPherson struts again in a simple arrangement reminiscent of that designed by Colin Chapman for the Lotus Elan. Unusually wide-based lower wishbones took care of both vertical and front-to-rear movement — a cheap but effective solution to providing an independent rear-end. Both front and rear suspension assemblies were mounted to the main steel monocoque body-chassis via rubber-insulated subframes. More than one technical journalist remarked on the apparent flimsiness of the structure that hangs the differential on the main hull and forms the rear mounts for

Test programme — Nissan engineers wanted to know what happened to a Z way beyond the limits of adhesion; not only how it behaved, but how well it stood up to a roll-over. This driverless tethered rig provided the answers.

Hot stuff for Japan only — the Fairlady Z432 with lightweight body is outwardly distinguishable only by the dull magnesium-alloy wheels and twin exhaust pipes. Some did duty as police cars.

the wishbones, but there was no denying that if it was up to the job, it, too, was a good piece of value engineering.

The Z's brakes were standard 10.7-inch discs at the front, while the finned alloy rear drums were from the 2000 Sports. Steering saw a welcome move from the SP and SR311's cam-and-lever to rack-and-pinion; a system which other Datsuns were to adopt, though most of them some long time afterwards.

So the design targets could be met. The ingredients were there, the engineering was inexpensive but not skimpy, the clothes were stylish and elegant. The production capacity was reserved and the price sector was set. On October 22, 1969, the Datsun 240Z Sports was announced in America.

The reaction was everything its planners could have asked for. 'For the money the 240Z is an almost brilliant car,' said *Car and Driver*. 'The difference between the 240Z and your everyday 3,500-dollar sports car is that about twice as much thinking went into the Datsun . . .' *Road & Track* called it 'the most exciting GT car in a decade', and later was to recall that 'more than one buyer merely read the details and rushed down to the nearest Datsun dealer, deposit in hand'.

The chances were that the dealer had a waiting list. Sometimes delivery took months and American buyers weren't used to that. Enough of them must have wanted the Z sufficiently, though, for they were still in short supply two years later, by which time 50,000 had been sold in the United States. That was to more than double in 1972.

By comparison, the Japanese home market for the car was small; for several years it did not amount to more than 5,000 cars per annum. Three Nissan Fairlady Z models were announced simultaneously with the 240Z launch in America but, mainly for taxation reasons, they had 2-litre engines. The Fairlady Z and ZL, which carried the factory code S30 and S30S, used the 2-litre L20 six-cylinder engine — a related unit to the L24, but with different bore and stroke dimensions and a maximum of 130 bhp instead of the 240's 150. The Z and ZL differed in detail trim and in the ZL's five-speed gearbox and lower final-drive ratio. The Z432 was a very different proposition. A 'homologation special' for competition, it had the S20 twin-overhead-camshaft 24-valve six-cylinder 2-litre engine that had been developed initially by Prince and used in the successful R380 sports-racing car. Outwardly, this 160-bhp PS30 model was distinguished by

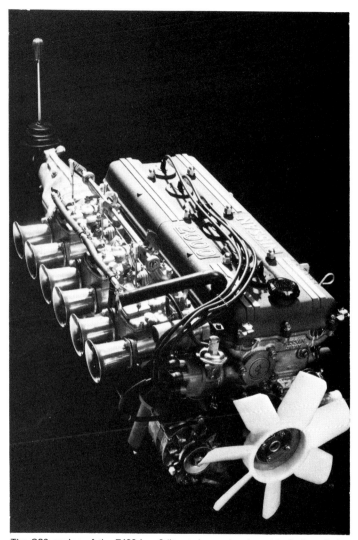

The S20 engine of the Z432 is a 2-litre twin-overhead-camshaft six-cylinder with 24 valves. Three twin-choke carburettors are part of the specification and there is also a special racing version. In street form the Z432 produces 160 bhp.

29

Heart of the matter. The strong L24 six-cylinder engine set the 240Z apart from its more feeble rivals and none at the price could match the Datsun's combination of modern style and performance.

magnesium-alloy wheels. It was not destined to be built in large quantities — only 420 were made in four years — and was not sold outside Japan. Apart from competition applications (the racing version, with three twin-choke Weber-type carburettors, was called Z432R) the Z432 was used by the Japanese police for highway patrol. The designation 432 is, incidentally, a simple one: 4 valves-per-cylinder, 3 carburettors, 2 camshafts.

The 240Z did eventually go on sale in Japan, two years after the initial launch, and with it came another competition version, the Fairlady 240ZG, featuring a number of parts that the company wanted to homologate for sports car racing. Most notable was the extended 'aerodyna' glass-fibre nose section. Apart from being 7½ inches longer than standard, the new nose closed in the normal radiator intake above the bumper and replaced it by a

Japanese competition model — the 240ZG has an extended nose section that blocks off the over-bumper grille and has an enlarged duct beneath. Headlamp scoops are extended and covered with transparent cowls (see Chapter 7).

deeper apron below to duct air. The visual effect of this rather impressive new front was spoilt by the ZG's crude bolt-on plastic wing flares, which were fitted to allow the use of wider wheels.

We come to Britain and Europe late in this account of the Z-car's launch since chronologically it was so. Cars went on sale in the USA early in 1970 and Nissan USA's sales figures show that 10,000 were sold in North America in that first year. But the Z-car didn't cross British shores until autumn 1970, with the arrival of the first car for exhibition at the October Motor Show and five rally-prepared examples that were to be used for the RAC Rally. Cars for sale did not come through until summer 1971 and then were in slow supply; the record shows that only 264 had arrived by year's end.

Part of the British importer's anxiety about the Z was the publicity its low price had received in America. As we have seen, it was a direct competitor to the MGB GT there. In those days the equivalent home price of British sports cars was actually lower than the US export figure. An MGB GT was £1,356; a Triumph

GT6, £1,287; TR6, £1,453; and Lotus Elan, £1,995. Though readily available in right-hand drive (the Japanese drive on the left, too), the cost of transport and distribution in Europe, and the relatively small volumes involved, plus extra taxation, meant that the 240Z could not be offered at a bargain price. It was first sold in Britain for £2,288, moving it up a class and in amongst such cars as the new mid-engined Porsche 914, the Alfa Romeo 1750 GTV and the home-grown Reliant GTE and Marcos.

As some compensation, the 240Z model, coded HS30, sold in Britain had the five-speed gearbox that the standard American-spec HLS30 lacked, as well as radial-ply tyres (on 4½-inch rims).

As a result mainly of the RAC Rally appearance, the Z was seen by British enthusiasts as a successor to the Austin-Healey 3000 that had ceased production in 1967. One of the rally team, trying the 240Z for the first time and finding it quite a handful on the loose, said that it felt like 'a big Healey before sorting'. Some road-testers did their best to destroy this idea — 'the only resemblance between the Datsun and the Healey is in having a

front-mounted six-cylinder engine', said *Motor* — but the comparison persisted. *Autocar* said: 'There's no denying that the character (of the Healey) is there . . . but the Datsun is so much more comfortable, so much roomier and so much better handling that comparisons are difficult. We would prefer to think of the 240Z as exemplifying what the MGC should (and might) have been.'

All agreed that it *was* the six-cylinder that set the Datsun apart from most of its rivals and, for all its old-fashioned flexible chassis and jarring ride, the Triumph TR6 was its closest competitor. It, too, had an in-line six-cylinder engine of 2½ litres, 150 bhp, and independent rear suspension. It also had closely comparable performance (0-60 mph and standing quarter-mile times within fractions of a second and a 119-mph maximum speed to the Z's 125) for nearly £800 less.

But the Datsun had the style of the 1970s, while the TR6 was the last throw for an old stager that went back to the 1950s. In 1971, Britain was only beginning to discover the difference. In America, the 240Z was already well on its way to overtaking the Chevrolet Corvette and becoming the world's best-selling sports car.

Transatlantic rivals — in Britain, the 240Z came closest in format and performance to the six-cylinder Triumph TR6 (above) while in North America the biggest-selling sports car was the home-grown Chevrolet Corvette (below). The Datsun was soon to overtake them both.

CHAPTER 4

240Z

1969-1974

Let's look in more detail at the 240Z in its original form. A strict two-seater with a fixed-head coupe body and an opening tailgate, its general configuration can be compared with that of the E-type Jaguar. In overall length, 13 ft 7 in, it is 9.5 inches longer than a contemporary MGB, but 0.3 inch shorter in the wheelbase, at 7 ft 6.7 in. Wider by 4 inches than the MG — and with a rear track a useful 6 inches wider than the old Datsun Sports roadster — it nonetheless contrives to look relatively narrow and high, even by the standards of the time. The very futuristic-looking Marcos, offered in Britain with a 3-litre engine at about the same price as the Datsun, was no less than 5 inches lower. One reason for the Z's height is a generous ground clearance — 6 inches plus — dictated by its international markets and, incidentally, very useful in rallying! Overall, its dimensions match the Porsche 911 pretty closely.

Given the need to keep weight down as far as possible, the anticipated production volumes, and the more sophisticated manufacturing equipment that was becoming available at Nissan, it was inevitable they would choose an integral body-chassis instead of a separate chassis-frame like the older Datsun sports cars. The rigidity of this all-steel hull depends on a welded structure that meets at the dashboard bulkhead. A massive box-section cross-member behind the seats forms part of the floor pan and there are major structural rails running forward inside the wings, acting as both engine and suspension mounts, and backwards from the rear cross-member to the rear bumper mounts. The roof panel is in one piece and no additional roll-over bar is built in.

The resulting structure is not particularly light by sports car standards; 20.4 cwt (2,284 lb) is the kerb weight of the British 240Z. Neither, despite its very streamlined appearance, did the Z's body provide a very impressive drag coefficient — 0.467 — though nobody cared very much about that in those pre-Energy Crisis days.

The MacPherson-strut front suspension takes advantage of the production economies that this system allows. The simple sub-frame, mounted on the body/chassis with rubber insulation, runs beneath (and supports) the engine and carries the pivot points for the pressed-steel lower links, while the long struts mount at the top inside turrets behind the wheel wells. Torque arms run forward from the main structure and are rubber-mounted — they look after braking loads and fore-and-aft compliance as the wheels ride bumps. An anti-roll bar mounted in front of the subframe is a standard fitting.

The use of MacPherson struts at the rear is less conventional. The Datsun's layout has been called a Chapman strut system because of the similarities to the neat and simple arrangement Colin Chapman devised for the Lotus Elan. The struts, with coil springs high up, mount inside towers that intrude into the Z's luggage area and pick up at the rear of the hub-carriers behind the drive-shafts. Location is by very wide-based lower wishbones that mount at the front to a cross-member that supports the nose of the differential and at the back to a subframe formed by two sheet-steel members that support the rear of the differential via rubber bushing. In the early cars the drive-shafts — they have two constant-velocity joints and a ball-bearing spline — trailed backwards from the differential by about 10 degrees; this angularity caused some problems and the differential cross-

Near the peak — *Autocar's* long-term test 240Z in Switzerland during a 1972 Continental sortie. An absolutely standard car from the British importers, the author drove it for 12,000 miles and had no mechanical trouble.

Looking through the Z — a cutaway drawing of an early British-market 240 shows the mechanical layout, including strut suspension front and rear, two-piece prop-shaft and underfloor location of the fuel tank and spare wheel.

member was moved back to make the drive-shafts align laterally from 1972 models onwards.

Girling brakes, made in Japan under licence by Sumitomo, are used, with 10.7-inch diameter plain discs at the front and 9-inch diameter finned alloy drums with leading and trailing shoes at the rear. Separate hydraulic systems operate front and rear and a Bendix vacuum servo is fitted as standard. A pressure-limiting valve is installed to prevent premature rear wheel lock.

The steering is rack-and-pinion — very unusual for a Japanese car at the time — and high-geared, with only 2.7 turns from lock to lock. Turning circle of 32 ft is good for the car's size.

Standard 14-inch diameter wheels are 4½J ventilated pressed-steel with four-stud fixing. British cars were all supplied with these, carrying a variety of ugly hub caps. Early, tinny-looking 'spoked' wheel trims were replaced by domed gunmetal grey ones with five scooped cut-outs which were unusual in being located in the wheel by a serrated edge all around the circumference.

All British-market cars were supplied with radial-ply tyres of

1972 British-specification 240Z showing rubber spoilers front and rear. 'Scooped' body-colour wheel covers are a great improvement on the earlier type, though still obviously 'hub caps'. The badging has been tidied up and circular motifs on the rear quarter-panels now double as air extractors. To meet local regulations, the indicator lights are mounted above the front bumper instead of within nicely moulded housings below the headlamps, but the front looks better without the overriders of the American version. Japanese-style wing mirrors on this car were not a standard fitting in Britain.

175 section, but almost all seem to have been fitted since with alloy wheels, often with wider tyres. In America, many were supplied with special wheels from the outset and the factory's 5½J magnesium alloy competition wheels were available there as an option.

So, leaving aside for the moment the Z's straight-line performance, and remembering that it is a conventional front-engine/rear-drive machine (with, surprisingly, very nearly equal front-to-rear weight distribution) how well does its all-independent suspension perform? Does it provide the comfort and the escape from the harshness of the traditional two-seater that its makers sought?

Not quite, was the consensus of opinion of professional testers when they got to grips with the first production cars. More than one remarked that, for an all-independent suspension car, the Z was very stiffly sprung, and made the more so by the high tyre pressures recommended — 28 psi all round. At low speeds the

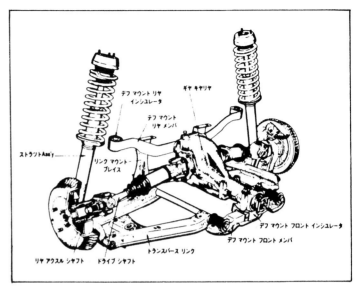

The independent rear suspension is more complicated, and differential chassis mountings look flimsy at a glance. MacPherson struts are used, as at the front, but with a wide-based wishbone each side. Drive-shafts are double-jointed and have ball-bearing splines. Drum brakes are finned to aid cooling.

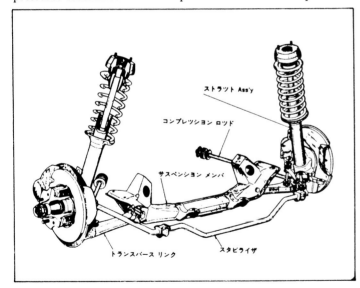

The front suspension (shown here as described in the Japanese manual) is straightforward MacPherson strut-type with lower links mounted to a simple subframe, torque arms from the main body/chassis, and a front-mounted anti-roll bar.

ride was universally condemned as poor and jolty. *Autocar* thought that it was over-damped rather than over-sprung, pointing out that as the car went faster the ride improved markedly. At high speed on a motorway it was pronounced 'very comfortable'.

There are certain types of road conditions that the rear suspension doesn't like, though — undulations, dips or humps taken at speed can catch it out. On the other hand, its performance over poor surfaces, producing, as it were, single-wheel bumps, is remarkably good. Whether by intention or coincidence, this characteristic was shared with the specially developed rally cars. The high ground clearance is also a help here, of course.

Bumps get transmitted pretty faithfully to the driver through the steering. Up to a point, this is as it should be, and this prominent 'feel' is a small price to pay for its high-geared precision. So is the undeniable heaviness at low speeds and when parking.

The strut suspension all round means that the Z's roll-axis is relatively high, so the car's roll-angles are small, even when cornering fast, and the wheels stay more or less vertical and in contact with the ground, providing what *Autocar* praised as 'very consistent handling characteristics'. Though pictures of rally cars on the loose create an image of the Z as an oversteering brute, under normal conditions its handling is on the understeer side of neutral, providing the driver exercises some moderation with the throttle. The car has more than enough torque to break traction at the rear on dry roads, let alone wet ones, but, driven smoothly, the 240Z corners very well indeed by the standards of 1971 cars. The writer took part in *Autocar's* two-car comparison test of the 240Z with the Alfa Romeo 2000 GTV (not the most obvious of pairings, but they were quite close in price and performance); we found that, given equal drivers, the Alfa could not stay with the Datsun over ordinary British B-roads, despite the Italian car's delightful, subtle handling. The Z's independent rear-end and its behaviour when the going got rough gave it the advantage and so did the grip of its wider 175-section tyres — Dunlop SP Sport radials in that case.

If oversteer is wanted, it is there by the bootful, and a skilled driver can use it to advantage and for his amusement. On dry, ·twisting roads it is fun to drive a Z-car 'point and squirt' — hard acceleration, brake hard in a straight line and balance the tendency to understeer through the corner by applying the power early. In the wet, the car needs more respect, and the front wheels will lose grip first. Again, the car can be balanced by the accelerator, but it requires a degree of finesse and it is very easy to generate a bigger slide than you bargained for by using a little too much throttle in a low gear through a tight, slippery corner.

In the safe confines of a closed circuit it is possible to generate the most lurid slides, as the writer found out when tyre testing at Silverstone with a 240Z. But, as ever, the quickest way was not the most spectacular and the best lap times were achieved by a more gentle balance between right foot and steering wheel.

Tyres are worthy of some further comment. The first cars that came to Britain were fitted with Bridgestone Speed 20 radials, which had much better wet grip than most Japanese tyres experienced up to that time, but produced a lot of road noise.

Later cars had Dunlop SP Sport CB73 Aquajet radials, appropriately HR-rated (rather than the Bridgestone SRs, which were theoretically unsuitable for the car's maximum speed) and made in Japan. They varied in their performance. *Autocar* praised those on their long-term test 240Z as being every bit as good in the wet and dry as the identical British Dunlops. Others, including a number of motor racing people who ran Zs — March racing car designer Robin Herd was among them — felt that the tyres were below par. It was discovered that the tread compound of the Japanese SP Sports had been changed and that later tyres were identical in composition to their British counterparts. That raised a potential problem for those seeking to buy replacement tyres, but it is now only of academic interest since most 240Zs will have gone through one or more sets of more modern rubber.

The tyre roar was less acute with the Dunlops, but still there, and road noise generally comes through quite clearly to the cockpit — a function of the open load area, which is not as well insulated as a separate luggage compartment would be. Also, most 240Zs seem to have some creaks and groans and other 'noises off' generated by the rear subframe and many have transmission whine — from both the gearbox in the lower ratios and the differential. The writer's 1972 car had such a noisy axle that early failure was expected, but in fact it quietened in 10,000 miles. The gearbox whine, on the other hand, increased. Provided the door seals are in good condition, wind noise is low up to about 115 mph when, rather alarmingly, internal air pressure pushes the door frames away from the sealing rubbers.

Discussion of noise brings us to the heart of the matter — the engine. It isn't inherently very noisy — much less so than some other sports cars of its era — but the roar of a passing 240Z has a purposeful note, and on the over-run can turn into an impressive bark. Again, one would expect many original-series cars to have non-standard exhaust systems by now and we know that the system can change completely the car's audible character; the factory rally cars with twin megaphoned tailpipes made a glorious, very six-cylinder, bellow, though it was of questionable legality!

Today, there doesn't seem anything particularly special about a single-overhead-cam engine with an iron cylinder-block and an aluminium-alloy head. In the early-1970s, ohc engines tended to be the reserve of up-market sporting cars. The cheaper British

Access underbonnet is good, and as such typical of Japanese cars of the period. There is room inside the wing alcoves, adjacent to the dashboard bulkhead, to accommodate the battery on one side and the windscreen washer reservoir on the other — hence the little flaps to enable access for topping up.

sports cars didn't have them because neither did the saloons that shared their engines. Well, the Datsun 510 Bluebird did, and as such had gained a reputation among the sports car set in America as something of a budget-priced BMW. The 240Z's L24 engine was basically the 510's L16 short-stroke four-cylinder with two more cylinders tacked on. For enthusiasts it had a head — and a lot of other bits' — start.

Actually there were more similarities with the 510SSS model than the 'cooking' Bluebird as the L24 shared the valve timing and valve sizes (1.65-inch inlet, 1.30-inch exhaust) and the 9:1 compression ratio of the hotter saloon. In America, Datsun enjoyed a reputation for powerful engines, though the figures themselves are rather misleading since they are gross SAE figures instead of the more realistic DIN nett outputs that are the norm today, but the 510 four-cylinder was quoted to produce an impressive 96 bhp at 5,600 rpm with a single carburettor. The

Japanese-market SSS, with twin carbs, was rated at 109 bhp. Despite its relationship with the more highly tuned of these two engines, the L24 compares pro-rata with the ordinary 1600 in delivering 150 bhp at 5,600 rpm. This was with the twin Hitachi-SU HJG 46W carburettors with 46-mm choke diameter (the SSS four-cylinder used 38-mm versions). The torque figure — an important factor in the character of the Z — is 146 lb ft at 4,400 rpm and this high maximum is complemented by a nice flat torque curve.

So the 240Z left plenty in reserve and promised unfussy performance and long life. As if to emphasize this confidence, the rev counter's red line was marked at 7,000 rpm — way, way beyond the power peak. It would go there without ill-effect, but in practice there wasn't much point in revving it so hard.

The valve train is pretty conventional. The camshaft is centrally placed and runs directly in the head in five plain bearings and is driven directly from the front of the crankshaft by a long double-chain-and-sprocket assembly. The cam operates the valves by forged steel rockers, which are kept properly located to the cam lobes by 'mousetrap' springs. The valves, which have double coil springs, are in line in the combustion chamber and tilted at 12 degrees from the cylinder bore centre-line. Intake and exhaust ports are on the same side — to the right, when viewed from the front. The combustion chamber is more-or-less wedge-shaped, and the pistons are flat-topped, cast aluminium, slipper-skirt type. The crankshaft is forged steel and rides in seven substantial 2.1-inch diameter bearings. Though in-line six-cylinder engines have less inherent torsional vibration problems than other configurations, the L24 had its share of crankshaft failures early in its US racing programme. Vibration periods showed up in normal road use, too, and all 240Zs seem to have rough patches through the rev range, sometimes aggravated by imperfect balance in the drive-line. At the top end — beyond 5,000 rpm in the experience of two cars that passed through *Autocar's* hands — it can begin to rumble uncomfortably. In practice, though, this is above normal change-up points or top-gear cruising speed. Under most conditions the L24 feels — and is — a strong, beefy engine.

It drives through an 8.8-inch single-dry-plate clutch directly to the gearbox — five-speed in the case of all British-market cars. An overdrive 'box with a geared-up fifth ratio of 0.85:1 and a direct-drive fourth, it has nicely spaced ratios that are well chosen to complement the engine's excellent torque spread. The latter allowed a high first gear and the ability to trickle along in top below 20 mph and pull strongly from that speed if desired.

With the 3.9:1 axle ratio of the five-speed car (American four-speed versions had completely different intermediate ratios and a 3.36:1 final-drive) the maximum speeds in the gears are:

1st	44 mph	(7,000 rpm)
2nd	69 mph	(7,000 rpm)
3rd	98 mph	(7,000 rpm)
4th	117 mph	(6,380 rpm)
5th	125 mph	(5,750 rpm)

These are from *Autocar's* 1971 test car. Their 1972 long-term test car pulled another 60 rpm in fourth gear, but was 4 mph down on maximum speed when checked after 10,000 miles. In both cases it is worth noting that the speedometer was about 5 per cent optimistic at 100 mph and it showed over 130 mph in top.

As the writer was involved in recording these figures it is appropriate to add a note here about straight-line stability. The 1972 car had the spoilers front and rear that became part of the UK specification in that second year, and it is significant that this car had better high-speed stability than the original 1971 car which lacked these aerodynamic add-ons.

A long fast journey on the Continent in 1972 had shown that 100 mph, or just 5,000 rpm in top gear, was a comfortable and realistic motorway cruising speed, which gave the Z very long legs indeed; the 'happy' cruising speed of most of its rivals was rather lower.

Against the stopwatch, the through-the-gears acceleration figures delighted even those who had examined the car's design and expected it to be quick; another tribute to its torque curve and well-chosen ratios. A 0-60 mph time of 8 seconds was slightly better than the contemporary Porsche 911T and Triumph TR6, and streets ahead of most other competitors. More to the point, it was only 0.6 second slower than the 4.2-litre Jaguar E-type and proportionately close to it over the standing quarter-mile with a time of 15.8 seconds. The Jaguar coupe had a much higher top speed — 140 mph — and, to be fair to it, was at the time tremendous value, for at £2,711 it was only £423 more than the Datsun.

Autocar's overall fuel consumption on road test was 21.4 mpg and their long-term Z in more normal use recorded similar figures. That car only rarely improved on 23 mpg, but with four-star at only 35p a gallon in 1972 it didn't seem to matter much!

US four-speed cars with their different gearing — but overall very close at 21.4 mph/1,000 rpm in top gear to the UK 21.6 — showed similar or slightly slower acceleration times and a maximum speed of around 120 mph. Though power output was rated the same for the US cars, when installed there was some power loss to drive the air pump that was necessary to meet the early exhaust emissions regulations. The pump injects air into the exhaust manifold to burn off hitherto intact hydrocarbons, but brings with it a valve system that upsets throttle response, both on and off, and makes smooth driving difficult.

Not that the UK version was always the smoothest around. Most cars seem to have a jerky throttle movement, rather sudden clutch take-up and a tendency for the prop-shaft universal joints to clunk unless the driver takes great care when moving off from rest. So it can take practice to make smooth low-speed gearchanges without jerking.

The five-speed all-synchromesh gearbox has an 'Alfa-style' change — now the norm for such boxes, but by no means so in 1970. First to fourth are in the conventional H pattern, with fifth alongside third to the right and reverse directly below the fifth-gear position. Like the steering and the clutch, the gearchange is heavy; it is spring-loaded to the centre, third-fourth, plane. Changes in the first-to-fourth H are precise enough, though engagement of first from rest can baulk, but the dog-leg into fifth is slower and it is all too easy to touch the unguarded reverse cog in the process.

The brakes are hard work, too, but do their job well. Check braking from low speed does not require undue effort, but for the ultimate stop, measured by *Autocar* at over 1g, 120-lb pedal pressure was needed — and that's a heavy push. But, just as the steering, the extra effort in the extreme case is compensated by

Interior layout of a 1972 British-specification car. Earlier 240Zs had a hand throttle matching the choke lever, just behind the gear lever, and a slightly different arrangement of switchgear. Legroom in the footwells is generous and the heater blower does not intrude, as it appears to in this picture. The degree of seat recline is limited by the luggage shelf.

excellent progression; the harder you push the better the stopping. *Car and Driver* in America were very critical of the first 240Z's braking in the wet and this was solved by fitting a different pad material.

Generally, though, the braking performance is in line with the Z's image as a hairy, gutsy machine that needs a man-sized effort to get the best out of it. What doesn't line up with that image is the automatic transmission that Nissan offered from October 1970 onwards as an option. A three-speed unit made by the collaborative efforts of Nissan, Toyo Kogyo and Ford in Japan, it was offered in the US for an extra 190 dollars as part of the sales pitch to the wider market. Not surprisingly, enthusiasts didn't go for it; in a reader survey of 106 240Z owners in 1972, *Road & Track* found that only two had opted for automatic transmission.

Inside story

It comes as something of a surprise to find that there is a lot of room in a Z-car until you remember for whom it was designed. Indeed, the car is much better suited to large people than small ones, like most from its home country. The 240Z has only two seats, but they have a tremendous range of adjustment and drivers who combine bulk and a 6 ft-plus height have no trouble getting comfortable. Shorter occupants, on the other hand, can find the seats too low and can feel very closed in by the high window line and unable to see the length of the bonnet. Spacers can be fitted beneath the runners to raise the seats up to an inch, but this was never a factory modification. British-market cars have reclining seats with quite a wide range of backrest adjustment (early US cars had only a 10-degree adjustment), but in practice, if the seats are quite well back on their runners the backs hit the bulkhead at the rear of the seat well. With the steering wheel set at an ideal angle, almost everyone can find the right driving position in a Z-car. The seats themselves are well shaped, but rather thinly padded, and have head restraints built in. These 'tombstones' may have a useful function in the event of an accident — and meet corresponding safety legislation — but they contribute to the claustrophobic feeling some have and certainly do nothing to improve rear vision, which is already restricted by the depth of the rear quarter panels.

The controls are well placed. The pedals — organ-type throttle

'Tombstone' seats were standard, thinly padded and not very nicely upholstered in early Zs. The door trim plastic matches them well, but mock-quilted plastic on the central tunnel does not, and cheapens the interior appearance. Note the inside door handle on the curved bottom edge of door — a convenient feature.

Down the hatch — the rear door opens high and is supported by a single gas strut. Luggage has to be lifted over a high sill, but once inside can be anchored by straps provided or wedged around the wheelarches and suspension-strut towers. The platform has a raised lip at the front to prevent luggage sliding forward.

and pendant brake and clutch — are ideally positioned for heel-and-toe operation, even for someone with small feet. There is a 'dead pedal' rest for the left foot, which is appreciated since the footwell is deep. The short gear-lever falls nicely to hand and the handbrake is alongside the driver's seat next to the transmission tunnel on right-hand-drive cars (left-hand-drive cars have it in the same place, *ie*, alongside the passenger seat).

The one-piece moulded facia has something of the Corvette about it, with deeply cowled speedometer and rev counter. Two combination gauges (temperature/oil pressure, ammeter/fuel) and a clock, also well recessed, dominate the centre of the dash and are angled towards the driver — a neat arrangement, but they need a deliberate look rather than a glance. The left-hand column stalk (right-hand in left-hand-drive cars) is a neat cluster including two-

speed wipers and washers and all the lights, while a thin stalk on the opposite side is for indicators and headlamp dipping and flashing.

The wipers, despite anti-lift arms, are useless above 90 mph. British-market cars from 1972 onwards had Lucas quartz-halogen headlamps fitted by the importers. Early cars had a hand throttle lever matching the choke on the centre console, but most have a choke only. UK specification included a heated rear window, operated by a little switch on the panel in front of the gear-lever, which covers the fuse-box.

The centre console includes a radio slot, a useful map light, a swivel ventilator and the heating/ventilation controls. Heating and ventilation are both good enough and the three-speed booster fan commendably quiet, but it is irritating that the two functions cannot be used together to give heat to the footwell and cold air at face level. The eyeball ventilators at either end of the facia do not adjust easily. A lot of US cars have air conditioning, not offered in Britain. Front window winders are close to hand above the door handles that are conveniently placed at the very base of the doors, where the bodywork side curves in. The rear quarter-windows do not open and air outlets for flow-through ventilation are provided in the rear pillars. Loudspeaker mountings are built in at the back of the luggage area, but are not ideally placed for stereo listening.

There is a lockable glove compartment in front of the passenger and a useful open tray on top of the transmission tunnel. The open luggage compartment can swallow a surprising amount and is easily loaded through a strut-supported hatch, and straps are built in to secure suitcases. The suspension strut housings obstruct the load area to some extent, but also form 'breakers' against which to stow smaller items of luggage. There are two

There is no room for anything but luggage in the rear of a 240Z, but beneath the carpet at the forward edge of the luggage area there are two concealed compartments, one of which houses the jack and tools. Grilles set into the trim above the strut housings are for air extraction; those at the extreme rear are badly positioned to accommodate stereo speakers.

Working out at Silverstone. Handling characteristics were praised by *Autocar* as consistent and predictable. A tidy line like this is quicker, if less spectacular, than generating lots of oversteer.

lockers within the chassis central box-section, immediately behind the seats, and these are reached by pulling back the carpet. The jack and tools live there, and the spare wheel is similarly concealed under the rear floor.

This kind of detail fitment had already become a Japanese hallmark when the Z was introduced, as had a well laid out engine compartment for routine service work. So these were expected, even in this most un-Japanese of Japanese cars. East-West differences in taste do show through, though, in the interior, which has too many different kinds of indifferent plastic materials, including some very cheap and cheerful mock quilting on the sides of the transmission tunnel. The steering wheel rim is wood-grained plastic, but the gearlever knob came from a tree.

The standards of exterior fit and finish were not universally impressive. Reports from America talked of the ease with which the big smooth wing and body panels could be rippled — even by

hand — while the paintwork of early cars was not all that durable, flaking readily around stone chips or minor parking scratches. In Britain, *Car* magazine was particularly critical of finish and quality-control aspects: 'Our test car had horrible groans, rattles and whines . . . having laid out the best part of £2,500 we would look sideways at some of the nasty plastic interior bits. . . .'

Running changes

The 240Z was sold until the end of 1973. By then some 190,000 Zs had been produced and 135,000 had been sold in the United States. Inevitably there were a number of detail modifications during that time, some of which have been covered in the description. The most major changes were at the end of 1971, for the 1972 model. The rear cross-member and the differential mountings were moved back 35 mm (1.37 inches) to reduce the angularity of the drive-shafts. Viewed from above, the

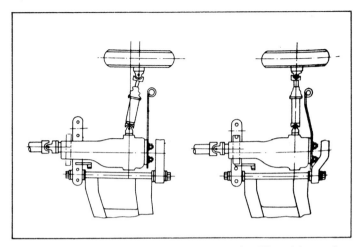

A question of angularity. This diagram shows how the differential mountings were modified to reduce the angle through which the drive-shafts have to operate. The change (right) was incorporated for the 1972 model year.

new arrangement made the drive-shafts parallel rather than angled backwards, as they were originally. A slight change in combustion chamber shape effectively lowered the compression ratio, a change brought about by increasingly tight emissions control regulations in the United States. A one-piece prop-shaft with a single universal-joint was also introduced in an attempt to cure drive-line roughness. From 1972, US cars had 5-inch rather than 4½-inch wide wheel rims.

For 1973, US emissions requirements meant modifications to exhaust and inlet manifolds to include exhaust gas recirculation and different model carburettors. By then, bumpers on these cars had to be extended to meet insurance-dictated Federal rules. This required some chassis strengthening at the mounting points and lengthened the car by 6.2 inches. New flame-retardant materials were used inside, these also being in response to US regulations.

The exhaust emissions rules were beginning to take their toll on the performance and driveability of the Z-car, and the 1974 requirements were going to make things worse. The big 240C Datsun saloon had recently been uprated to 2.6 litres, but there was some reluctance to do the same with the Z because the extra capacity came from a longer stroke and made the engine less able to rev and therefore rather less sporting. But the American problem was a pressing one — and besides, there was another new, bigger and heavier variant to be considered that would further widen the Z-car's horizons.

CHAPTER 5

260Z & 280Z, 2+2

1974-1978

Once again the new model made its public debut at the Tokyo Motor Show, and once again the domestic model, powered by a 2-litre engine, was called a Fairlady — the Fairlady Z 2/2. For export it was to be the 260Z 2+2 and would go on sale in March 1974. The two-seater for overseas markets had already become the 260Z.

Lengthening the stroke from 73.7 to 79 mm increased the new model's engine capacity to 2,565 cc. Lengthening the car by 12.2 inches provided room for two reasonably sized seats in the back of the new 2+2 and thus brought the possibilities of Z-car ownership to an even wider audience.

The 2+2 'stretch' was unusual. Lots of manufacturers had given their sports cars vestigial rear seats by modifying the inside of existing models and others had produced different body styles to provide extra seating capacity. Nissan retained the Z's front-end intact, extended the wheelbase by a foot and restyled the doors, rear body and roof to accommodate the extra length. In doing so they lost some of the tight sportiness of the original Z shape, but there is no denying that the major modification provided much better rear seat accommodation than could have been possible within the standard 90.7-inch wheelbase.

The wheelbase was actually increased by 11.9 inches to 8 ft 6.6 in, the overall length went up to 15 ft 5.4 in, while the 2+2 was also 0.8 inch wider and 0.2 inch higher than its two-seater counterpart. Individually contoured rear seats have their backs at just about the rear axle line and with the front seats in the median position rear passengers have 9 inches of knee-room. Because of the extended high roofline, head-room is 2 ft 11 in, or nearly the same as in the front. The seats themselves are quite comfortable, but front passengers have to compromise on leg-room if adults are to be carried any distance in the back. But the rear seats are ideal for children or for use on occasional short journeys with four adults up, and that was the intention in widening the range with the new model. The rear seat backs are in one piece, which can be folded down to extend the load platform; easily done, providing a bigger luggage area than the two-seater's, and accessible through a similarly-sized tailgate. The 2+2 has quite different rear quarter-windows, which open for ventilation unlike the two-seater's, and longer doors, making entrance to the rear fairly easy. It's easier to get in on the passenger side, though, since only that front seat has a release that does not upset the backrest rake setting when tipped forward. Sensibly, the doors have interior release catches front and rear.

Nissan proudly claimed that all this had been achieved with the addition of only 1 cwt to the car's weight. In fact the difference between the kerb weight of *Autocar's* test 2+2 and the 260Z two-seater tested three years later was just 77 lb. The more telling comparison was with the 240Z, which showed just how much fat the Z had put on over the years — at 20.4 cwt it was a full 3 cwt lighter than the 2+2. And whilst the claim that the 260Z 2+2 and two-seater would have comparable performance was justified, the expected improvement over the 240 was not borne out in tests.

Mechanically, the 2+2 is the same as the 260Z two-seater, with the obvious exception of a longer prop-shaft. The longer wheelbase does produce an improvement in ride quality in general, though it also increases the rear suspension's proneness to bottoming over long undulations.

The Z's handling was scarcely affected by its elongation into a 2 + 2, but the larger 260 engine could not compensate in performance for the car's extra weight.

The 260 2 + 2 does not have the purity of line of its two-seater counterpart. The doors are longer and the roof reprofiled, giving it a squarer look and a less flowing tail. The differently shaped rear quarter-windows hinge open, unlike those of the two-seater. Revised rear panel treatment, including separate reversing lights, was new for the 260Z and was shared by both models.

In Britain, the initial price of the 2 + 2 was £3,499, £602 more than the two-seater. In America, the price had gone up to 6,000 dollars for the 2 + 2.

The vagaries of emissions regulations make the L26 engine story somewhat confusing. Maximum power of the bigger engine was up on the 240. Using the gross SAE figures, a 12-bhp increase to 162 bhp at 5,600 rpm was claimed. At the same time,

From the front, or examining the facia, as is the author here, there is nothing to distinguish the 2 + 2 from its two-seater sister. The proportion of 2 + 2s sold in the US was initially about a quarter of the number of two-seaters, but rose steadily. In Britain, more customers appreciated the extra seating, and in 1975 more 2 + 2s were sold than two-seaters. The latter disappeared from the British market for a while, but even when it did reappear the 2 + 2 comfortably out-sold it.

A change in the appearance of the carburettors identifies this as a (European-model) 260Z, but otherwise the underbonnet scene is familiar to 240Z owners. Electrical components have been tidied up and there is extra pipework associated with EEC emission control equipment, though it is minimal compared with what was needed on US cars of the same era!

however, Datsun started to quote more realistic net horsepower figures, which gave a peak power value of 150 bhp (DIN) at 5,400 rpm. A comparable figure for the L24 was 130 bhp (DIN). According to literature published by Datsun UK Ltd at the time, the compression ratio of the L26 was reduced to 8.3:1, so that the Americans could make use of low-lead and therefore lower-octane fuel, and in Britain it could run on three-star 94-octane petrol. But the American publicity for the new model talked of the engine size being increased 'to prevent loss of power as a result of complying with 1974 emissions regulations' and an 8.8:1 compression ratio, like the latter-day 240Z. And to make things even more complicated, power output of the American model was rated by the new SAE nett measurement procedure at 139 bhp at 5,200 rpm. An 11-bhp difference between the de-toxed US version, with its exhaust gas recirculation, air pump and so on, and the European model does seem plausible. There are similar discrepancies between the quoted torque figures, but both the 152 lb ft (SAE gross) UK-spec and 137 lb ft (net) US-spec at 4,400 rpm are somewhat higher than comparable figures for the same markets' 240Zs.

As the larger engine produced its peak power at lower revs than its predecessor (that isn't in dispute!) the overall gearing was raised slightly by changing the final-drive ratio from 3.9 to 3.7:1. To complete the picture, fifth gear was lowered from 0.85 to 0.864, so that the mph per 1,000 rpm in top gear went up only from 21.6 to 22.6. Of relevance here — though it made little difference to the gearing — was the new tyre equipment, 195/70 low-profile VR radials on 5-inch rims.

So, given more power, more torque and better matched gearing, the 260 ought to have been as good a performer as the 240Z, even allowing for the extra weight, but most found it not to be the case. In a test of the 260Z 2+2, *Autocar* found that the maximum speed was 5 mph down (at 120 mph), 0-60 mph was nearly 2 seconds slower at 9.9 seconds, and it took 1½ seconds longer over the standing quarter-mile (17.3 seconds). To its chagrin, it fell to the bottom of a comparison with the Alfa Romeo 2000 GTV, Ford Capri 3000 and Reliant Scimitar GTE, all of which offered similar accommodation at a significantly lower price.

Some of the reasons for bigger not being better lie in the L26's unwillingness to rev as freely as the L24. The 2.6 would not go beyond 6,800, and even then gave warning of valve bounce, and neither fifth nor fourth-speed maxima reached the peak of the power curve. Clearly, the 260Z's engine did not have the broad power band of the earlier car and fell away sharply beyond the peak. Disappointingly, there was not a compensatory improvement lower down the rev range and *Autocar* reported that although the new unit was smooth and tractable it was 'noticeably lacking in punch'.

There was one saving grace — an improvement in fuel consumption from 21.4 to 23.9 mpg overall. A typical figure for the 260 was around 25 mpg, which was important in the early days of 1974 when the shortages of the first Fuel Crisis were uppermost in people's minds and a 50 mph 'economy' speed limit had been imposed in Britain. It wasn't the easiest of times to promote a new sports car!

It isn't surprising to find that the Z-car sales graph — until then a steep upward climb — took a dip in 1974. The 2+2 was intended to widen the Z's appeal and therefore to win additional sales. We cannot know whether this would have happened if the fuel and general economic situations had been different. As it was, total 260Z sales in Britain in 1974 amounted to only 60 per cent of the previous year's figures for the 240Z. Sales went down even further in 1975. By then, Datsun UK were doing very big business with their bread-and-butter saloons and the 260Z was an expensive and relatively specialized car which threatened to divert their dealers from the everyday traffic in Cherrys, Sunnys and Bluebirds. Z sales in Europe generally were so small — Britain, France, Germany and Holland bought only 600 between them in 1974 — that the factory decided to concentrate on 2+2 sales and by 1976 the 260Z two-seater had virtually disappeared from these countries' showrooms.

In America, the numbers were not down as much and in its first year the 2+2 took almost a fifth of the Z's total of nearly 50,000; this proportion was gradually to increase in the years that followed to nearly 30 per cent by 1977.

Datsun UK's records show that only 356 two-seaters were sold in Britain in 1974 and 1975 and all of the models delivered in 1976 were 2+2s, so those early 260Zs have a rarity value, even if they don't quite have the performance of the more numerous 240. The two-seater was to come back to Britain in 1977, though even then only in limited numbers; the total of right-hand-drive 260Z two-seaters for the British market was less than 900.

In America, the 260Z didn't last much more than a year before it became the 280Z. That was a product of increasingly demanding US exhaust emissions regulations. Leaner ignition settings and more and more add-ons had made the carburettor six-cylinder engine temperamental. It didn't go as well as it had to begin with (though the Datsuns were not alone there), could be difficult to start, was prone to hesitation and erratic throttle response and to 'surging' at steady speed on the freeway. Besides, the opposition were catching up. . . .

The final stretch to the L28 engine's 2,753 cc was made by a 3-mm increase in bore to 86 mm. One imagines that there was

In Japan, the 2+2 was known as the Nissan Fairlady Z 2/2 and the standard model continued with a 2-litre engine. In other respects appearance was similar to export models, but Japanese regulations called for wing mirrors instead of door-mounted side mirrors and, despite various attempts to style them, they spoil the Z's clean lines.

The Japanese-market Fairlady 260Z two-seater for 1977 adopted alloy wheels as standard; these were also to be used on British-market cars when the two-seater returned. Zs for Japanese consumption continued to be badged on the front and sides simply 'Fairlady Z' and they have a small Nissan badge on the tail, with no mention of Datsun.

Well-shaped rear seats in the 2 + 2 were more comfortable and the car provided more room there than one might expect, though they are more suitable for children than for adults on long journeys. They can also be folded forward to extend the luggage area. Exit from the rear compartment was helped by repeater door handles near the trailing edge of the doors.

required from the late-1970s onwards. A flap in the air intake measures airflow to the engine, and transducers also read throttle position, engine rpm, air and water temperature. This information is fed to the computer, which generates electrical pulses to open needle valves at the injectors and admit fuel for a measured amount of time.

Engine modifications didn't end there. Combustion chambers had to be opened-up to match the larger bores, and the compression ratio was lowered (for certain this time!) to 8.3:1. Inlet ports were enlarged and inlet valves increased in diameter to 1.74 inches and a new camshaft was fitted with less duration and overlap. The result of all this work was a horsepower increase to 149 bhp (SAE nett), 10 up on the 260Z measured by the same system, more torque (163 lb ft at 4,000 rpm) but, much more important, better driveability.

The 280Z was an immediate improvement on the fussy US-spec 260 and late-model 240Z. *Car and Driver* summed it up in a June 1975 test: 'Fuel injection delivers the best of all worlds: legal emissions, excellent fuel economy (20.5 mpg on our mileage cycle), good driveability and respectable horsepower. Right now, the 280Z has the technology it needs to motor through these trying times. . . .'

Road & Track were not quite as fulsome in their praise, finding that response from low speeds and light throttle openings was still poor. They also remarked on a clunk from the drive-line caused by a switch in the injection system that cut off fuel on the overrun between 3,200 and 2,800 rpm.

But the 280 hadn't regained all the 240's lost performance. With the US-standard, but now closer-ratio, four-speed gearbox test figures showed 0-60 mph at between 8.3 seconds (*Car and Driver*) and 9.4 seconds (*Road & Track*), a standing quarter-mile in around 17 seconds and a maximum speed of 117 mph. It was quite a lot faster than the 260Z and now not far away from the contemporary Corvette — which had also suffered emissions strangulation over the years.

The 280Z was carrying a lot more weight around than its ancestor. The massive Federal bumpers with shock absorber mounts were bulkier than ever in their definitive '5 mph' form, and with a catalytic converter system (in 1975, required for California only) the car had a 200-lb weight penalty compared with 18 months before, and at 25.6 cwt was nearly 5 cwt heavier

long thought about the advisability of this for it left only a single transverse water passage between the centre two cylinders. Its success is proved by its adoption for Z-car's successor, the ZX, and for Datsun's big saloon and estate car. At the same time, the SU-Hitachi carburettors which were proving all-but-impossible to tune in line with the emissions regulations, with the resulting starting and durability problems, were replaced by fuel injection. The US 280Z was among the first users of the Bosch L-Jetronic electronic injection system made under licence by Nissan and Diesel Kiki. This kind of computerized system has since become more commonplace, mainly because of the very precise metering it can provide — all-important in achieving the very low levels of emissions that US (and some other countries') regulations

The 260Z 2 + 2 with two of its six-cylinder companions in the 1977 Datsun UK range — the Laurel 200L, which used the 2-litre six and, in the background, the big 260C estate car that shared the Z's 2,565-cc power unit, but with only one carburettor and 118 bhp.

The 260Z two-seater in the final form in which it was offered in Britain. Sales continued well into 1979, after the ZX had been introduced, and Datsun UK's records even show two new car registrations in 1980!

This Japanese-market car shows that the 260 retained a similar dashboard layout to its predecessor, but the centre console has revised heater controls, twin air vents and some extra warning lights. This one also has remote-control wing mirrors operated by little joysticks on a panel to the right of the steering column.

By 1977, the Z used much better interior trim than the first 240s. Carpet extends up the transmission tunnel sides and the seats have corduroy cloth centre panels. As if to point to its position at the top of the Datsun range, mock wood strips run along each door panel, but the plastic-wood steering wheel rim has given way to plastic-leather.

than the original 240Z in US spec.

Spring rates changed quite considerably over the years to cope with this extra weight and the front struts were actually bigger in diameter on the 280, while the steering, never light, began to require man-sized muscles. 'What started as a truly sensuous machine had taken a serious turn towards the macho,' said *Car and Driver,* who went on to praise the greater precision of the handling on its wider 195/70 tyres and condemn the brakes as marginal for their weightier task. There was also some criticism of the steering when running straight ahead. A vagueness was put down to too-soft rubber bushing mounting the rack to the front cross-member, a problem that had affected earlier Z-cars. (The solution was to shim the bushings to increase their preload against the rack).

Outwardly and inwardly the 280Z was scarcely distinguishable from the 260Z that preceded it and which continued to be sold elsewhere; the 280Z was purely for North America. It increased

the marque's popularity there to a high-spot of 70,000 cars sold in the US in 1977.

American versions still lacked the front and rear spoilers of European-spec cars, but otherwise these later models can be identified from 240Zs by their wider wheels, different rear lamp clusters with separate reversing lights, and the matt grey rear body panel.

Inside, there are only detail differences from the original car. Standard all-black trim replaces the ill-matching shades of brown plastic in some earlier Zs. Carpet covers the transmission tunnel and spring turrets instead of that cheap quilted vinyl, and the doors are adorned with narrow strips of imitation wood. The steering wheel rim is padded and covered in leather-look plastic in place of the wood grained variety. The centre console has two adjustable air vents instead of one and revised heater/ventilator controls (now illuminated) which enable the driver to select hot air to the footwells and face-level fresh air, and the wipers have an intermittent setting. In Britain, a radio/cassette player with an electric aerial became standard equipment in the 260Z; in the US the list price included an AM/FM radio.

The 260Z 2 + 2 was well established by the time the two-seater made a popular return to Britain in September 1977. By then the 260Z had increased in price from £2,898 at its announcement to £5,728; the 2 + 2 was £6,530, and it found itself with an altogether more formidable set of rivals. Cars like the Porsche 924 and Triumph TR7 had appeared, bracketing the Datsun between them on price, and both produced in recognition of the Z-car's success in America. The newly announced mid-engined Lancia Monte Carlo had the same order of performance and only a slightly higher price, while in Britain, specialist cars like the Ford V-6 engined TVR also represented direct competition.

The formula that had mildly disappointed 240Z devotees when the 260Z was first put to the test began to seem inadequate when the two-seater came up for reassessment at the end of 1977. *Autocar* had at least expected it to be quicker than the heavier 2 + 2 and were surprised and slightly confused when their apparently well-fettled test example was not. A maximum speed of 115 mph and 0-60 mph acceleration of 10.1 seconds didn't compare well with the 127 mph and 8.8 seconds that *Motor* had recorded for the two-seater in 1975, and certainly didn't look good amongst its new competitors. The TR7, over £2,000

The tailgate of the 260Z is supported by two gas struts to avoid distortion and aid positive closure. Black vinyl trim and matching carpet provide a more luxurious and better co-ordinated look to the interior. Despite changes to the rear panel, the big British registration plate does not quite fit the space provided and needs illumination from above and below (the lower number-plate lights are a UK-market feature).

cheaper, was nearly as accelerative and the 3-litre Capri could still knock spots off it.

The Z was still a fast car by most standards, of course. Its fuel consumption was good for a 2½-litre car, averaging 25 mpg. Fuel tank size had increased from the 240 and earlier 260's 13.2 to 14.3 gallons (15.9 to 17.2 US gallons). There had been a gear-ratio change during the model's absence, the final-drive having been raised again to 3.55 (23.6 mph/1,000 rpm in fifth) and first and second lowered; the gearing was now the same as the US 280Z. A viscous coupled fan became standard with the 260, but contributed more than it should to the noise level. In other respects, the Z had become much more refined than the earlier model; it remained a satisfying driver's car which turned the

heads of passers-by. The trouble was that too many passers-by could be in 'lesser' cars!

As in America, British testers found that the brakes were less than impressive now that the car had gained in weight. Hard use, as in concentrated fast driving on winding roads, could fade them and heavy braking set up a disconcerting rumble. Initial pedal effort was lower than the 240Z, suggesting the use of softer pad and lining material. Sterner stuff was recommended for anyone who expected to use the 260's performance to the full.

Autocar summed it up like this: 'If there had been no 240Z one would be less inclined to criticize the 2.6-litre version. The fact is that, seen as a proper sports car, the newer model offers less than the earlier one'.

What was happening was a move away from the out-and-out sports car to a softer, more civilized Grand Tourer. The Americans had already praised the new (optional) air conditioning of the 260/280 with its four-speed blower as a near rival to the GM system that set the standard for air conditioning. Their proportion of Zs with automatic transmission was rising and there was a call for power steering. Moreover, the price in the US had gone up steadily until, by 1978, it was around 9,000 dollars and far removed from the bargain sports machine the 240Z had been. Mazda had introduced the neat Wankel-powered RX7 to fill that gap. It was a couple of thousand dollars cheaper than the 280Z; Datsun decided not to compete with it but to move the Z-car up-market. Though some had been misled by the appearance at

Exhaust-emissions regulations became increasingly tight in Japan, too, where the 2-litre engine was fitted with fuel injection as part of Nissan's emissions-control package known as NAPS. The badging on this home-market car proudly indicates the fitment of this cumbersome set of devices.

motor shows of a small mid-engined Nissan sports prototype, unofficial sketches of a wider, more voluminous coupe showed the way the Z was due to go.

The original Z-car had redefined the sports car. In less than a decade 550,000 had been sold, making it easily the most popular sports car in history. Though some enthusiasts were disappointed that its replacement was to be more 'GT' than 'sports', by 1978 Nissan had a good idea of what was needed to maintain and expand the Z's market in the future. The world had changed since 1969 and the new car, the 280ZX, needed to reflect that. Nissan spelt out their philosophy: 'With the goal of achieving harmony between human society and the automobile, as well as between each individual and his vehicle, the development concept of the 280ZX represents an attempt to breathe substance and form into an ideal image of a sports car which both responds to the multitude of social problems surrounding the automobile and offers its owners what they truly desire. . . .' In other words, it meets all the regulations and we think people are going to like it!

CHAPTER 6

Getting fat — 280 ZX

1978 — 1983

When the ZX did appear some people hardly noticed the difference. It was unveiled in Japan as the new Fairlady Z in August 1978 and widely regarded as simply a facelift of the existing Z-car. Europe saw the 280ZX first at the Paris Motor Show in October, but no special effort was made to launch it to either Press or public. Indeed, with Japanese car sales in France being low-key, the ZX was grouped in a tightly packed stand to one side of the main exhibition hall. At first glance the newcomer — a 2+2 — looked like the familiar 260Z. During the show's Press preview, journalists asked each other, 'is there something different about that?'.

The 280ZX received a better showing at the first Motor Show at the National Exhibition Centre in England a couple of weeks later, though its arrival took even Datsun UK by surprise — they hadn't known that the factory was going to send the car until a few days before the show opened. European sales were not due to start until the following Spring.

America got the new models in November 1978, which was only fair since the demand for a new Z was manifestly greater in the US than anywhere else. This time the car was a product of extensive market research and the involvement of the Nissan US company, which has its own Product Planning Department in California. Manager of the Product Development Group, Englishman Peter Harris, says that the Japanese were 'incredibly co-operative' in producing the kind of car that the US company felt was needed. He explains: 'We were out of the market for a purist sports car; we wanted to make it more a GT. Performance, handling — yes — but with a lot of comfort; power windows, cruise control and so on. A US 'personal' car. We got what we wanted.'

According to Nissan in Japan, the form of the new Z-car was based on the results of four lines of research — satisfaction and dissatisfaction with the earlier model; what people *expected* a new Z to be like; energy conservation and regulations; and new manufacturing technology. The outcome coincided with the feeling of the US sales people that they wanted a more luxurious, more comfortable version of the same. Japan described it as a 'new song on the same theme'.

That was to understate the amount of work that had gone into the new car. The styling similarities that were to give Z-car owners that warm family feeling disguised the difference under the skin. The ZX was not a facelift. It was a new car from the ground up, with only the engine and transmission as a direct carry-over from the previous model.

Dimensions were all different. In most respects the ZX is bigger than the earlier Zs and certainly bulkier. For some — for whom the original 240 was the Z-car ideal — that made it less attractive. But it was part of the appeal to new customers; those who might be trading down from a Cadillac or a Thunderbird, making the gesture of 'thinking small'. Even so, American journalists were surprised by the sales pitch at the ZX introduction. *Road & Track* said it '. . . could almost make us believe we'd been time-machined back to Detroit pre-1976, the date that saw the first of the new breed of smaller and more people-, package- and fuel-efficient cars coming from US automakers . . . Spewing from the mouths of Datsun executives were words like: longer, lower, wider; and softer riding, quieter, more refined; and full colour co-ordination, all-new this and all-new that; and a new Grand Luxury package, bringing the ZX to new heights in luxury. Incredible.'

It was, and is, most of those things and the differences are more apparent comparing the European rather than the US specifications, for the Federal-bumpered Z-cars were 10 inches longer than their European counterparts. One of the objectives of the ZX was to incorporate these regulation requirements in the overall design, so a US 280ZX two-seater is just an inch longer than a 280Z and the 2+2 is actually 3 inches shorter in its new form. The various versions compare thus:

	240Z	260Z	280Z (US)	280ZX	260Z 2+2	260Z 2+2 (US)	280ZX 2+2
overall length (in)	163	163	173	171/4*	175	185	179/182*
Overall width (in)	64	64	65	66.5	65	65	66.5
Wheelbase (in)	90.7	90.7	90.7	91.3	102.5	102.5	99.2
Track (in)	53.5	53.5	53.5	55.0	53.5	53.5	55.0
Height (in)	50.5	50.5	51.5	51.0	50.7	50.7	51.2
Kerb weight (lb)	2300	2555	2875	2660/*2825	2630	2850	2850/*2990

*US-spec ZX is 3 inches longer in each version than European cars because of bumper overriders; greater weights for US cars are predominantly due to emission control equipment.

Overall, the two-seater is longer, has a longer wheelbase, wider track and greater width than its predecessor. The 2+2 is some 4 inches longer than the old car with normal bumpers, but on a wheelbase that is 1.3 inches shorter; it is similarly wider in stance. In European trim, the ZX is slightly heavier than the Z in two-seater form and significantly so when comparing old and new 2+2s. Nissan, it seemed, were being extravagant at a time when others were looking to size and weight reduction, but that was the American market strategy.

There were some useful steps forward. The ZX was the first Datsun to be thoroughly tested in a wind tunnel during the design stage. The reprofiled nose and bonnet with its integral bumper and front spoiler and clean body sides brought the drag coefficient down from the 0.467 of the first Z to a respectable 0.385. The coefficient of aerodynamic lift is much improved from a value of 0.41 for the earlier car to 0.14 for the ZX, while there is a similar comparative improvement of performance in yaw — which on the road relates to side-wind stability.

Though weights had gone up, Nissan took some pride in the fact that the ZX wasn't heavier still. A number of areas of

Surprise revelation — the single 280ZX 2+2 on the Datsun stand at the 1978 Paris Motor Show. Though it had been announced in Japan earlier in the year, not much information about the new Z-car had come to Europe, and it was not clear that there would also be a two-seater version of rather different appearance. In fact, ZXs were not offered in Europe, or in the USA, with the steel wheels of the show car, which come from the basic Fairlady Z sold in Japan.

Nissan's designers went from ideas sketches to one-fifth scale clay models to arrive at the ZX shape. These show variations on the theme at a fairly early stage and are interesting in their different glass depths and headlamp treatments.

bodywork, particularly around the dash-panel, were strengthened, while almost all of their other objectives for the ZX, from the higher level of equipment to the quest for noise reduction and greater refinement and the provision of a bigger (18-gallon) fuel tank, resulted in added weight. Significant savings were made, they say, in the weight of the body structure itself.

Z cars have always had a close to ideal 50:50 weight distribution, but to retain that with the new design meant moving the engine rearwards. The car's configuration, then, is slightly different from its predecessor and the floor pan, like the body, is

new. One can detect that Nissan's engineers are disappointed that the two-seater has to have as much overhang at the rear as it has with that drooping tail, but they explain that not only was it necessary to accommodate fuel tank, spare wheel and luggage, but also there were American rear-end collision regulations to consider. Those requirements also dictated moving the driver's seat forward by 3 inches and presented quite a problem to the designers trying to preserve the Z's long bonnet outline. The solution they arrived at included angling the windscreen more steeply, bringing its top rail 1½ inches further back.

A very large number of fifth-scale clays were made and some were wind tunnel-tested. Findings there suggested refinements of the lines as well as limiting the air intake to below the bumper. Finally, three designs were adopted for further development — models A (top), B (centre) and E (above).

Of the final fifth-scale models, proposals A and B went forward to full-scale clays and after much deliberation the rectangular-headlamped A was rejected in favour of B with a front end reminiscent of the Z (left). But in the final run-offs in the design department, a latecomer, design C, which was similar to B but without the side panel indentations, was adopted. It went through fully equipped full-scale clay models to metal prototype and eventually to production prototype (right). The whole ZX styling process took three years.

One effect of the ZX's arrival was to separate the two-seater and the 2 + 2 more than they were before. With the original 2 + 2 the rear seating space was achieved simply by lengthening the wheelbase of the two-seater. For the ZX the cars were designed in parallel, rather than one developing from the other. The result is a completely different shape for the tail, rear quarter window and roof line for the two versions.

Though *Autocar* was unkind enough to say that the ZX 2 + 2 looked like 'a 240Z that had been frightened by a Toyota Celica' (in marketing terms in America that may not have been too far from the mark!) many think that the bigger body is the more successful of the two ZX styles. Certainly it is the one that better fits the character of the new model.

The 2 + 2's square-cut tail carries the drip channel to the point of the rear quarter window. Inside, thanks mainly to some 3 inches of extra cabin width, there is claimed to be 15 per cent more rear seat room. The rear seats are further back than in the equivalent Z and are now above the rear suspension; the seats fold down individually. More space there may be, but it is still pretty restricted for an adult.

The Z gave little cause for complaint in its front seat accommodation, but the ZX sought to improve it. Legroom remains more than adequate for tall people, but the extra inside width of the 2 + 2 and 1.2 inches extra in the two-seater gives a little more shoulder space to the sides. On both models the hatchback door is bigger than before.

Though there are detail differences all through the mechanical specification, the one major change is the rear suspension. Partly as a move towards improved refinement and comfort, but mostly in the interests of manufacturing and servicing economy, Nissan adopted semi-trailing arms for the ZX. This is the same system as used on the contemporary 810 saloon, giving a neat twist to the American advertisements which had promoted that six-cylinder model as the 'sedan with the 240Z engine'.

The Nissan cutaway drawing of the 280ZX US-market two-seater is as exquisitely complex as the under-bonnet layout. Features that can be clearly seen include the strut spring/damper units, the disc brakes, front and rear, and the intake air filter mounted in front of the radiator — the only place it could be accommodated in such a crowded scene!

DATSUN 280ZX

The ZX's suspension is still mounted on a subframe, itself joined to the underbody via rubber bushing. The pressed-steel semi-trailing arms are of the conventional kind used by BMW, Ford and others for their big saloons, but the pivot axes are nearer to purely 'trailing' in Datsun's case. There is an anti-roll bar at the rear. Despite its relative complexity, the semi-trailing-arm layout is not as theoretically effective in controlling wheel angles as the Z's rear struts.

MacPherson struts are retained at the front, but now with tension rods (leading arms) going forward from the suspension uprights to the nose underbody. The front anti-roll bar diameter is increased to 22 mm and larger diameter springs are used (150 mm).

In the quest for running refinement, a good deal of attention was paid to cutting down unnecessary friction in the shock absorbers and rubber bushings. Nissan claim more than a 25 per cent reduction in friction in the dampers compared with the Z by changing the shock absorber oil seal and the viscosity of oil used

The front suspension of the ZX is a conventional MacPherson-strut layout, though different from the Z in having tension rods running forwards to pick up on the main body structure. The lower links are mounted on the subframe crossmember.

The rear suspension is quite different from the Z in having semi-trailing arms instead of wishbones, and the whole structure is supported by a massive subframe. The design is shared with Datsun's 810 saloon. Note that the rear brakes have solid discs while those at the front are ventilated.

and improving the smoothness of the piston rods.

Different springs are needed for the front of the two ZX variants, but they achieve the same rate of 126.6 lb/in, while at the rear there are three types of springs for different versions and specifications of the two-seater and two for the 2+2.

The Z's rack-and-pinion steering was retained for the new car. The steering gear ratio was reduced (3.5 turns lock to lock instead of 2.7) to lower the effort needed for low-speed manoeuvring, but with increased car weight compared with the later Zs, a major complaint about which was heavy steering, the new optional power steering was expected to be fitted to the majority of ZXs. This sounds like a retrograde step when described as a recirculating-ball system — the Z had positive rack-and-pinion when most Japanese cars used recirculating balls — but in fact is one of the best power-assisted systems available, being made in Japan under licence from the German ZF firm. It provides

variable assistance, for light steering effort at low speeds and good road feel at high speeds, where the power assistance is reduced. It retains the Z's tight 2.7 turns from lock to lock.

It is generally agreed that the power steering is the best choice for the ZX. It was standard in Britain on both models, in any case, and in America standard on the 2+2 and optional for the two-seater. The unassisted rack-and-pinion has not benefitted much from the work applied to it; effort required is still man-sized, and response, spoilt on later Zs by too soft rack bushings, remains poor. The ZF power steering receives general praise. In normal driving it is not too light and has good feel and accuracy for an assisted system. Indeed, the ZX's handling is good by any standards. There is just the right amount of understeer to give the car good stability and reassuring cornering under most conditions. A gentle shift to oversteer is made when lifting off during hard cornering, but it is easy to catch. Thanks to

195-section radials (Michelin XDX in the case of European-market cars) there is plenty of grip and *Autocar* summed up the 2+2 by saying: 'It is capable of surprising cornering speeds for its size . . . being a comparatively long car it gives the driver very good feel of what is happening — this is a highly impressive aspect of the 280ZX which we greatly enjoyed.' *Road & Track* admitted that their skid-pan and slalom test readings gave the ZX better results than the 280Z, but more subjectively on the road found more understeer and slower steering response than before.

American versions have been criticized for their soft ride — *Road & Track* said that there was not enough control on rough roads for their taste — but here different specifications for different markets confuse the issue. *Autocar* said of the 2+2: 'Overall, the ride is firm; it isn't by any means a soft-riding coupe, although like many cars with the same sort of suspension character, the ride improves with speed'. This is an area of judgment that is very subjective, where standards of hard and soft vary and normal road conditions have an influence. In the writer's view, having driven ZXs on both sides of the Atlantic, the US-spec car (which is a good deal heavier than the European car)

lacks the tautness of that sold in Britain.

Bearing in mind the criticism of the brakes on later and heavier Z cars, Nissan went to discs all round for the ZX with 10-inch ventilated rotors at the front and 10½-inch solid discs at the rear, upon which the handbrake also operates. A larger 9-inch servo (previously used only on the Z 2+2) is standard, as is a proportioning valve designed to prevent premature rear-wheel lock. In fact, tests suggest the brake balance to have gone too far the other way, with the front wheels locking rather earlier than is ideal. This, in fairness, is a problem that affects quite a lot of cars because of the criteria used in the regulations on brake performance both in Europe and the USA. *Autocar* reminded that such front-end bias could and does bring fade problems in repeated use — like travelling fast down a winding mountain pass. Even so, the system is a distinct improvement over the marginal brakes of the later Zs.

The unchanging part of the ZX was the engine, though even this was new to Europe as the 280Z had been developed for America. With licence-built Bosch L-Jetronic electronic fuel injection and breakerless electronic ignition (mounted on the

Aerodynamics didn't play a part in the design of the original Z, but by the mid-1970s the emphasis on fuel economy made a good drag coefficient important. Extensive wind-tunnel testing with the ZX brought the C_d down to 0.385 and improved stability. A key to its good aerodynamic performance is the unbroken line from bumper to windscreen; indeed, the gap between bumper and the front edge of the bonnet is positively sealed.

The 280ZX two-seater in American specification has small bumper overriders that British cars lack, but is in most other respects very similar to models sold elsewhere. The ZX body was designed to incorporate bumper systems meeting '5-mph' US regulations.

A 2 + 2 in action in Germany. Wheels adopted for European-market cars are the same as those for the US two-seater. Note the considerable difference in overall shape of the two-seater and the 2 + 2, though they are the same from the screen forwards.

The 280ZX sold in Britain was very fully equipped, including such items as headlamp washers, with nozzles discreetly built into the headlamp scoops. Once again the big British number plate does nothing to improve the smooth styling and aerodynamic cleanliness of the nose.

distributor), the ZX's standard L28E power plant was similar to that used in the US 280Z. Once again power ratings are confusing. The Japanese specification quotes 145 bhp, but the European market cars are rated at 140 bhp (DIN) while the SAE (nct) figure for the original US/Canada specification, which included Exhaust Gas Recirculation (EGR), but a catalytic convertor for California only, is 132 bhp. Compared with the earlier car, the exhaust manifold is modified and a different kind of viscous coupling is used for the radiator fan as part of the bid for noise reduction.

As before, five-speed manual gearboxes and a Jatco three-speed automatic are available, the latter for the first time on a Z car in Britain. Gear ratios and final-drive (3.7:1) remained the same as the 260Z for European-market cars and the GL in America;

standard final-drive in the US is 3.36:1 (24.9 mph per 1000 rpm in top) while automatic-transmission models for all markets have a 3.545 axle.

From a performance point of view the 280ZX two-seater with manual gearbox proves a touch faster than the US 280Z laden with all its Federally mandated equipment. According to *Road & Track's* figures, 0-60 mph takes 9.2 seconds and maximum speed is 121 mph. *Autocar's* for the comparable European-spec car are 9.8 seconds and 112 mph. An automatic 2+2 proved, not surprisingly, to be slower at 0-60 in 11.3 seconds and a maximum 111 mph. Those maxima suggested that the European ZX was slightly under-geared and that the higher final-drive ratio of the US manual-transmission cars is the more efficient choice.

Certainly, the fuel consumption of the *Autocar* 2+2 auto wasn't

The crowded underbonnet of the European 280ZX remains reasonably accessible, though extra items like the power steering pump confuse a previously simple layout. Cold air to the fuel-injection system enters via a duct in front of the radiator and passes through a filter set across the low nose.

If the European car seems complicated, look at this one! It is a 1980 American 280ZX, and although all the major items are familiar (brake servo and battery have been transposed for this left-hand-drive car and the battery itself is a sealed one) the demands of anti-pollution legislation have produced yards more pipe and wire.

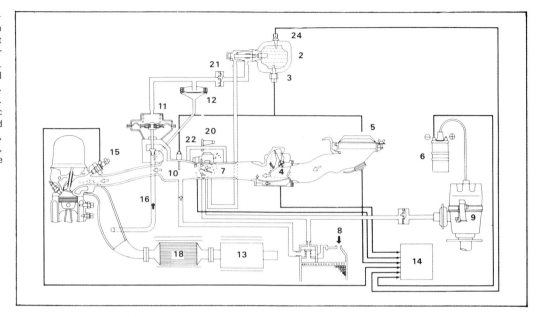

Diagrammatic explanation of emissions-control system for US-market cars with key to components: 2, thermostat housing. 3, thermostat time switch. 4, air flow meter. 5, air cleaner. 6, coil. 7, throttle valve switch. 8, feed from fuel tank. 9, distributor. 10, cold start valve. 11, exhaust gas recirculation (EGR) valve. 12, BPT valve. 13, silencer. 14, electronic control unit. 15, injector. 16, recirculated exhaust gas. 18, catalytic convertor. 20, air regulator. 21, vacuum delay valve. 22, throttle chamber. 24, water temperature sensor.

all that impressive — 18.4 mpg over a 1,000-mile test with best intermediate figure of 19.3. The manual car was even more thirsty. *Road & Track's* manual five-speed two-seater gave a 'normal driving' figure of 26 mpg (Imperial).

On the road, the ZX is pleasingly quiet, especially by comparison with other sporting cars. Not only is it well insulated from mechanical noise, but the aerodynamic work has paid off in the very low level of wind noise. The engine is still not the quietest and smoothest, and has rough patches through the rev range as well as signalling 'enough' at 5,500 rpm (though the red line is way over the 5,200-rpm power peak at 6,400). Unfortunately, both differential whine and the transmission clunk that comes back through the drive-line from the rubber-suspended subframe, are still features of some examples, though neither are as generally marked as before.

Overall, the ZX does meet its objectives as being a smoother, easier to handle, more comfortable Z-car. *Road & Track* quoted Tom Wolfe: You can't go home again. 'Today's Z car is not yesterday's Z car and though purists will mourn the passing of the

sports car Z, enthusiasts will rejoice for the GT Z. The base coupe (two-seater) makes a feeble attempt at being the sports car that it once was. As that it's a sham. Adding the Grand Luxury options, however, totally transforms the car. In this guise the ZX makes no pretence at being something it isn't.'

A different proposition, and made so, for the Americans anyway, by the level and quality of equipment provided. The GL in the US was 'fully loaded' with everything from four-speaker component stereo to cruise control, power windows and remote-control mirrors. Much of that equipment comes as standard in the single models of the British range.

And in the market at which the ZX is aimed that equipment is important. Nissan put a lot of effort into the new interior and the facia layout, and the range of information it provides must count as among the best in a sporting car. The seats are good and different for the two-seater and 2+2, the former having a new version of the high-backed 'tombstone' bucket seats of the Z and the 2+2 providing lower backs with adjustable head restraints. Rear seats of the 2+2 are comfortable enough and realistically

The neat new facia — this is a Japanese-market 280ZT with automatic transmission — has everything one could wish for. Big major instruments in a binnacle in front of the driver and three supplementary dials angled from the centre of the dash are a development of Z ideas. The water-temperature and fuel gauges (with a second scale for the last quarter of the tank) share the main nacelle. The monitor-light system of British and US models has a tiny screen between the main dials. The wide console has room for a variety of radios and stereo tape-players.

Thin seats of the Z have given way to thicker, more fully upholstered ones in saloon-car style. Velour-type cloth trim is used on most ZX versions. The rear seat backs fold down individually to extend the load space, but legroom in the back is more restricted than before.

well padded at the front of the cushion to suit the high-knee position that adult passengers need to adopt. Seat materials — velour-type cloth or a nice knitted fabric in the higher-spec versions — are an improvement over the early Z's plastic and the seats themselves can have not only front and rear and reclining adjustment, but also seat height and pitch control and adjustable lumbar support.

Though the impression inside is of quality and complete furnishing, the space available somehow doesn't match up to the extra indicated by the tape measure. There is more width, but then there is more door furniture — armrests, pockets and so on — and the seats are bulkier. Anyone expecting the civilized Z-car to have more room than the old one is likely to be disappointed, and that particularly applies to luggage space. The Z carried its spare wheel under the rear floor, but the increasing size of both wheels and fuel tank meant that there wasn't enough room there in the ZX. The answer for the US market was to fit a Space Saver

A snag — the UK-specification 280Z 2 + 2 had a full-sized spare wheel before the adoption of a Dunlop Denovo and it had nowhere to go other than on the floor of an already restricted luggage area. US and other markets offer a collapsible 'Space Saver' tyre that squeezes into the side of the luggage bay. The parcels shelf linked to the tailgate struts can be removed altogether.

On the limit at the MIRA Proving Ground in England. *Autocar* found the 280ZX 2 + 2 was capable of cornering speeds that surprised them for a car of its size and type and that the handling was nicely predictable through the transition, shown here, from understeer to oversteer.

71

spare with an inflation canister in a compartment at the right-hand rear wing covered by a plastic panel extending from the spring housing to the tail trim. The use of such tyres has been of questionable legality in Britain and so the UK-market cars carried a full-sized spare wheel flat in the rear compartment with a neat plastic cover. The result, with the new 'parcels shelf' fitted to hide the contents of the luggage area, is such a small space that carrying a suitcase would be out of the question. Indeed, there isn't room for a briefcase between the spare wheel and the shelf and scarcely room for a reasonable-sized squashy bag alongside it. The shelf is removable and the back seats of the 2+2 fold down, of course, but unless you are prepared to risk travelling without a spare wheel the built-in luggage straps on the boot floor will hardly be of use. An obvious if expensive solution, and one which Datsun UK later adopted, is to fit Dunlop Denovo 2 run-flat tyres.

The new facia moulding is massive and presents a very clear instrument display with two big and impressive dials, flanked by two more and with three angled ones at the centre of the dash, rather like the old Z. The main dials are the speedometer and rev counter, and they are surrounded by the water temperature and fuel gauges. The latter in some models has a two-phase display with a second calibration below the main one giving a more accurate indication of the fuel level when less than a quarter of a tank remains. At the centre are a split oil-pressure/oil-temperature gauge, voltmeter and clock (digital with stopwatch and date in later models). All are very clear and easy to read and illuminated with a restful red glow at night. Controls, including the heating and ventilation ones, are well labelled and illuminated.

A little panel between the speedometer and rev counter is the ZX gimmick. The central warning system operates sequentially each time the ignition is switched on. A red light and then a series of symbols indicates that it is monitoring light bulbs, coolant, battery and screen washer reservoir fluid levels. At the end of the check, if all is well it flashes up a green 'OK' light; otherwise the red light remains on and the driver can pin-point the fault by depressing the check button.

One disadvantage of this impressive array of in-car information is that the central ventilators for the heating/ventilating/air-conditioning system are small and the side ones rather narrow and therefore more useful for demisting than air freshening for the occupants. There isn't really enough through-flow for effective ventilation in hot weather, even with the fan running or the air conditioning in operation. Things are improved by opening the rear quarter-windows, as one can on the 2+2.

Not many, it seems, agreed with my own assessment after first driving a 2+2 automatic in summer 1979. In an *aide memoire* to the *Autocar* road-test department I concluded: 'Altogether too big

The ZX image — Nissan's US advertising emphasizes 'Luxury in the Fast Lane' in an attempt to attract owners of Cadillacs and other expensive conventional saloons.

a lump of a car for its performance and aspirations. Hasn't really made progress'. It was just what the American market wanted and in its first year sold 78,000 there. Similar figures followed for 1980 — and those against the car-buying trend. An interesting breakdown of Nissan USA's research for 1980 shows that 66 per cent of ZX buyers were male, 62 per cent were married, 84 per cent lived in urban or suburban areas and that buyers had an average salary of 42,000 dollars a year. The ZX ranged in price from 10,350 to 14,300 dollars at that time, the top price being for the smart black and gold '10th Anniversary' model. According to the US marketing department, 75 per cent of sales were of the two-seater and almost the same proportion — though not necessarily with the same cars — chose manual rather than automatic transmission.

American buyers also went for the first major revision of the ZX — the optional T-bar roof. This was first seen on the Datsun stand at the 1979 Frankfurt Motor Show, where a 280ZX 2 + 2 appeared with the suffix TT. The first T referred to the removable smoked-glass roof panels — the centre buttress and the rear body hoop forming the T-bar. This was an arrangement increasingly favoured by the American manufacturers since it avoided the strengthening that was inevitable if an integral-bodied car was turned into a full convertible. In the ZX's case the conversion was quite simple with frameless side windows and the B-pillar forming a natural 'break' point and the rear bodywork staying intact. The second T stood for Turbo and indicated a 180-bhp turbocharged engine. Sadly, neither option was for sale in Europe at that time, but the T-bar roof went on to the US options list for the two-seater for the 1980 model year. By the end of 1980 orders for it were nearly 50 per cent of all ZX sales!

The T-roof panels are easily removed by pulling a lever that contracts a locating bar front and rear. When not in place they can live, but take up rather a lot of the restricted space, in the luggage area in a vinyl pouch. The effect is a cross between a full wind-in-

The T-bar roof with two removable smoked-glass panels was first seen at the 1979 Frankfurt Motor Show. This exhibition car was designated 280ZX 2 + 2 TT — the first T standing for the roof, the other for its turbocharged engine that was not to appear in production until some months afterwards. It also had a rear deck spoiler not unlike those fitted to the Zs.

T-bar version of the US 280ZX GL — the fully equipped model that comes with almost every conceivable extra. With the roof panels removed and the windows down, the driver and front seat passenger can enjoy the benefits of a full convertible. The panels are easy to fit and remove.

In the land of the Z-car — North America — they produced a special edition in two-tone black-and-gold for 1980 to celebrate the 10th birthday of the Z. The T-bar roof and all the GL equipment was joined by leather seating and a numbered plaque on each car.

The eagerly awaited 280ZX Turbo was described as a '1981½' model as it came on to the American market. Outwardly, the Turbo — available initially only as a two-seater — has different bonnet louvres and distinctive alloy wheels of 15-inch diameter with ultra-low-profile tyres.

the-hair convertible and a big sunroof, depending on whether the windows are wound down or up. Triumph Stag owners will feel at home, though the Datsun differs from the Stag in not having a drop-down rear section. As a result, rear passengers do get buffeted at speed with the roof panels off. It is rather nice when travelling alone just to take off the one side panel; reminiscent of the half-zipped tonneau covers of sports cars past.

The T-roof also became available for the 2 + 2 for the 1981 US season and on both models in Europe later that year. By then the Federal ZX had been given a power boost. Modifications to the emission-control equipment, notably the use of a three-way catalytic convertor, meant that the all-States 1981 ZX gained an extra 13 bhp, giving it a maximum of 145.

The version with significantly more power — the Turbo — went on sale in America in March 1981. It was available initially only as a two-seater with a T-roof and other optional equipment, including automatic transmission. At nearly 17,000 dollars it was 25 per cent more expensive than the GL two-seater.

More and more complicated — the underbonnet area of the Turbo shows identification on the cam box. The Garrett AiResearch turbocharger is tucked down on the far side of the engine. The close proximity of components means a risk of heat build-up, hence the shielding in various places and the flat nozzles crossing the engine, which are designed to play air on to the injection system and prevent fuel vaporization when starting hot.

A rather surprising amount of work went into this new model. Not only did the engine require modifications beyond the installation of a turbocharger; Nissan recognized that a substantially quicker ZX might benefit from suspension and steering changes, too.

So the Turbo's engine has slight differences in cylinder-head, pistons, intake and exhaust manifolds and camshaft timing. It has a larger radiator and an oil cooler — not normally fitted to the ZX. As the black box comes to rule more and more cars, Nissan took the opportunity to use centralized computer control for the fuel injection, ignition, idling speed and exhaust gas recirculation system. It has one of those technical sounding epithets that the Japanese car makers love — ECCS: Electronic Concentrated Engine Control System.

As with most turbocharger installations, the compression ratio is lower than the normally aspirated version. It drops from 8.8 to 7.4:1 and is accompanied by a knock sensor mounted on the engine block to avoid the damaging effects of detonation to which US low-octane lead-free fuel makes such engines prone. Power rating is 180 bhp at 5,600 rpm and the 203 lb ft of torque at 2,800 rpm is a massive improvement over the standard US-spec car's 156 lb ft at 4,000 rpm.

The turbocharger itself is mounted down to the left-hand side of the engine. It is a Garrett AiResearch To3 unit, made in California, with an integral waste gate set at 7 psi; the outer casing and plumbing are by Nissan.

This car was first available only as an automatic, mainly for ease of emissions certification, but also because a torque convertor irons out the lag of a turbo, and, it is said, because the five-speed gearbox would be marginal for the extra torque in its standard form. As it was the Jatco automatic needed beefed-up input and output shafts and other modifications.

High under-bonnet temperatures are a problem with turbocharged cars and are the reason for one of the few pieces of positive identification on the Turbo body — the NACA duct running into a louvred panel on the driver's side of the bonnet. (Apart from the badges the other I-spy clue is twin exhausts.) Like the Audi 200T and Quattro, the ZX Turbo has an auxiliary fan to blow cold air over the injectors to avoid premature fuel vaporization and aid hot starting.

The rest of the world knows it as the ZX, but in Japan the car is still known as the Nissan Fairlady Z. This model is the Fairlady ZT 2BY2 with 2-litre 130-bhp engine. Alternative versions are known as ZL and simply Z, and there are 280s with the same trim and equipment, but none of them are called Datsuns . . . and none are tagged ZX.

Changes to the running gear were rather more subtle. Though it had not really been a cause of complaint on the ZX, it was decided to fit a power-assisted *rack-and-pinion* steering system to the Turbo and this, like the rear suspension, was common to the 810 saloon — and developed not by ZF in Germany, but by Nissan in Japan. Spring rates front and rear are actually softer, but shock absorbers stiffer, considerably so at the rear; the front anti-roll bar is increased 1 mm in diameter while the rear one stays as the standard ZX.

Perhaps more important is the extra work done on the rear suspension rubber bushes, which are also stiffer than on the regular ZX. The net result of all this is a more positive feel, accompanied, thanks to the roll bar and damper changes, by less body movement both in roll during cornering and dive in braking, but without a serious effect on ride comfort.

Tyres are bigger, too, and on distinctive 6J alloy wheels of 15-inch diameter, being Bridgestone Potenza of ultra-low-profile P205-60.

Not everyone was convinced that the suspension changes were totally successful, but after being perplexed by what had been done, *Road & Track* proclaimed that the ZX Turbo's tauter handling was a significant improvement over its normally aspirated counterpart and summed up their road test thus: 'The ZX Turbo is one of the most exciting and satisfying cars we have driven in years'.

The Turbo's performance has a useful boost. 0-60 mph in 7.4 seconds is quick by any standards and a maximum speed of 129 mph makes this the fastest production Z car, and remember, this is with automatic transmission. The Turbo engine will run up to its 6,400-rpm red line without complaining roughly like its sisters. The turbocharger begins to have an effect at around 2,500 rpm but, as planned, the torque convertor ensures that the increased power is delivered smoothly. Maxima in the intermediate ratios are 50 and 85 mph.

The first allocation of ZX Turbos to the United States was limited to 1,000 a month and there was a rush for them! For the 1982 model year the 2+2 Turbo became available and so did the five-speed gearbox, though the automatic remained an option, as it does on the normally aspirated cars.

The 280ZX Turbo was never sold in Britain but did appear, rather belatedly, in the main left-hand-drive European markets and in Canada. While it was eagerly received wherever it was sold, Nissan's home customers were not offered the Turbo option. Though speed limits and other restrictions had little effect on the sale of performance cars in the US, in Japan there is a feeling that sports cars are in some way anti-social. Whilst two-seaters are not exactly banned there, they are certainly frowned upon, and ZXs, like Mazda RX7s, are usually sold on the home market in 2+2 form. Not that there are all that many of them. The Japanese market has not figured strongly in this story, for since the start the Z-car has been primarily an export product and the numbers sold at home are minuscule in comparison with those sold in the United States of America.

The 2-litre Z-car lived in Japan as the Fairlady Z. Like the 280 it had electronic fuel injection and the L20E 1,998-cc six-cylinder engine developed 130 bhp at 6,000 rpm. According to Nissan information at the time of introduction, this version of the ZX came in its most basic form with a four-speed gearbox, but this transmission option has not appeared in the catalogue. In any case the 2-litre five-speed had a much lower final-drive ratio (4.375:1) and 175-section tyres. Emissions regulations applying from 1978 on required the use of a three-way catalyst and Nissan's NAPS computer-controlled emissions control package in Japan. The Fairlady Z, ZT and ZL were offered alongside the Fairlady 280ZT and ZL and the 2BY2, which is the domestic name for the 2+2. As ever, the nomenclature is complicated. The factory type numbers for the ZX series are S130 and GS130 (2-litre) and HS130 and HGS130 (2.8-litre). The previous Z series were simply S30.

But everywhere other than Japan knew the fatter, softer, weightier, but very logical successor to the Z as the ZX. The new model, marked and previewed by a new engine in July 1983 and announced that autumn, was a development of the same theme and carried the same designation.

CHAPTER 7

New power unit

V6 — plus Turbo

By the 1980s, the Z's tough straight-six engine was getting old. Turbocharging wasn't enough to make what was very like a 20-years-old Mercedes-Benz power unit a proper competitor with the more sophisticated engines being offered by Nissan's rivals for their sporting cars.

Toyota, whose six-cylinder Supra had become a serious competitor for the ZX, concentrated on twin overhead camshafts and four-valves-per-cylinder heads. Nissan had done all that early in the Z history, during the 1970s' Japanese obsession with 'muscle cars'. The solid L-series engine was not a suitable candidate for extensive further development.

Besides, with production of more than 6,000 cars a month, the ZX was a mass-production model. We have already seen how, increasingly, the Z came to share components with other cars in the Nissan range. Big as its production is — in sports car terms — the company would be reluctant to tool-up for an all-new engine for just one model. Detroit had shifted from V8s to small V6s — all the better to install sideways with front-wheel drive.

Though Nissan's C-series saloon, which had always shared engines with the Z, remained conventional with front-engine, rear-wheel drive, there's no doubt that their engineers were looking to future adaptations when they designed the new power unit for the ZX.

So the new engine, announced first in the 300C 'Tokyo Taxi', the Cedric, was to be a compact V6. This fuelled rumours that the replacement for the 280ZX would be a smaller coupe in the European supercar mould. But, just as at the time of the first Z's replacement, enthusiasts' dreams did not coincide with Nissan's marketing approach in the United States. The new engine was a much more dramatic change than the car that it powered.

Nissan are known to have looked long and hard at existing V6 engines. Of particular interest was the all-aluminium 'Douvrin' V6, a co-operative project between Peugeot, Renault and Volvo and used in those companies' big saloons as well as the Alpine and De Lorean sports coupes.

In the event, they chose to copy neither the aluminium block nor the 90-degree configuration of the PRV V6. They did, however, aim to produce the world's lightest production 3-litre engine. At 370 lb it is some 45 lb lighter than the L28 straight-six and well below the Toyota twin-cam six, although, interestingly, it is heavier than the Rover V8...

Aluminium was used for some prototype blocks, but discarded on cost grounds. Finite element analysis enabled the cast-iron block to be made with the minimum of material compatible with the expected stresses and strains. So much so, in fact, that a special main bearing 'cradle' had to be devised in which all four main bearing caps are cast as a unit, with a frame connecting them.

It is certainly compact. The block is only 15.3 inches long and the engine overall is about half an inch shorter than Nissan's CA18 straight-four. The cylinder banks are inclined at 60 degrees, which means that the overall width of the engine is no greater than the straight-six with all its peripherals — important, as it turned out, to ensure that the Cedric saloon didn't jump into the next domestic tax bracket for wider luxury cars.

Used in conjunction with 120-degree spacing of the crankpins, the 60-degree vee layout achieves even firing intervals. It does, however, limit bore and stroke, as the pistons from each bank are close to each other at the bottom of their travel. Nissan decided that

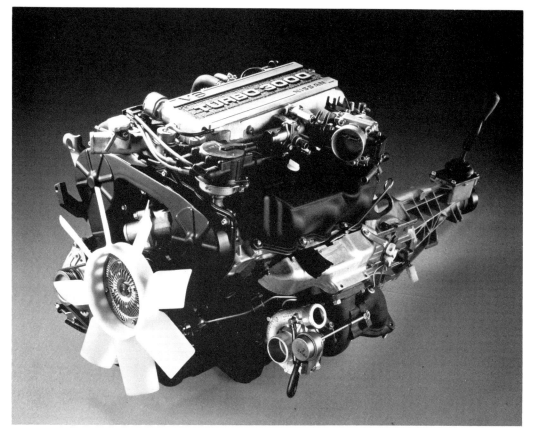

Turbocharged VG30ET engine has a distinctive cast-aluminium plenum chamber in the centre of the vee with a red top panel matching pressed-steel cam covers. The turbocharger sits low down on the left-hand side and is a relatively simple installation without the charge air intercooler of Nissan's more recent turbo rivals.

it was the best arrangement despite a need — for familiar reasons — to have both 2-litre and 3-litre versions. It means that the two engines have completely different bore and stroke dimensions, necessitating not only different crankshafts, con-rods and pistons, but also taller cylinder banks for the bigger engine.

Both engines are over-square: the 2-litre has a bore and stroke of 78.0 and 69.7 mm, the 3-litre 87.0 and 83.0 mm. The crankshaft is a nodular iron casting with five counterweights — competition-orientated Z-owners raised eyebrows at hearing this, but were assured that a forged crank would become available — and the con-

rods are steel forgings. The pistons themselves have short skirts and flat tops, save for some small cut-outs at their perimeter for valve clearance.

There are no fancy four-valve systems here, simply two per cylinder inclined at an included angle of 50 degrees and offset to one another so as to create a swirl effect in the pent-roof combustion chamber. The valves are actuated by a single overhead camshaft per bank, via neat little hydraulic tappets and cast-aluminium rocker arms. Camshaft drive is by a toothed belt running in a simple triangle with a central tensioner, while the oil pump is gear-driven

Cross-section of the V6 engine shows the 60-degree configuration, chosen because of the even firing intervals it provides with a 120-degree crankshaft. The engine is usefully compact, both in width and overall length, and is designed for low maintenance with, for example, hydraulic tappets that require no adjustment.

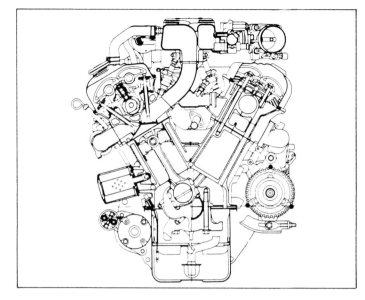

from the nose of the crankshaft and the distributor from the front of the left-hand camshaft.

Clearly, the VG engine — as the series is called — was designed for strength, durability and easy maintenance. The latter is looked after by the hydraulic tappets, which eliminate the need for valve clearance adjustment, and special materials for cylinder-heads and their gaskets, which mean that cylinder-head bolts never need retightening. Given that it was intended from the outset to be available in turbocharged 3-litre form (and, if needs be, turned into a diesel, though not for the ZX!), the 2-litre engine obviously has major reserves of strength. That smaller engine is unlikely to emerge from Japan in the ZX.

The Japanese-market 2-litre version of the new Z-car has a turbocharger as standard. With 1,998 cc, its power output is quoted as 170 bhp at 6,000 rpm, with 159 lb ft torque at 4,000 rpm.For export markets there is the choice of a normally-aspirated or turbocharged 3-litre: 2,960 cc, also producing a maximum of 170 bhp (at 5,600 rpm) with fuel injection alone (VG30E), but boosted to 228 bhp (at 5,200 rpm) in the turbocharged version (VG30ET). Corresponding maximum torque figures are 175 lb ft at 4,400 rpm

and 242 lb ft at 3,600 rpm. The 3-litre turbo is also available in Japan. As ever, cars for the American market, meeting the full gamut of emissions regulations, are less powerful: 160 and 200 bhp for the normally-aspirated and turbocharged 3-litre models.

Turbo versions have a compression ratio of 7.8:1 instead of the 9.5:1 of the normally-aspirated model, thanks to concave rather than flat pistons. The turbocharger unit is basically a Garrett AiResearch To3, as used on the 280ZX Turbo, but with Nissan housing and controls. Maximum boost, controlled by an integral wastegate, remains at 7 psi.

A piezo-electric knock sensor comes as part of the Turbo package, but there has been no attempt to cool the charge air with an intercooler, or water-cool the turbocharger unit as in the more recent systems of several of Nissan's high-performance rivals.

The electronic fuel-injection system is more or less a carry-over from the 280ZX, using the same Bosch/Nissan hardware, though with very different plumbing and the added sophistication of a hot-wire airflow sensor instead of the previous flap valve. The intake plenum, beneath the cherry-red engine top-plate, is clever, being divided down the centre and fed from the throttle butterfly at the

The underbonnet area of the 300ZX is still crowded, despite a tidier engine package — though the V6 allowed mounting further back and thus a lower front body-line. The engine's crossflow layout is the most logical arrangement for a V6. In this 300ZX Turbo, the air conditioning pump adds to complexity.

rear. The incoming flow alternates from left to right, corresponding to the opening of the inlet valves, and creates ram pulses which are said to improve low and mid-range torque by as much as 5 per cent.

The turbo VG30ET has a version of the Nissan ECCS electronic engine management system first seen on the 280ZX Turbo. For the USA, Japan and other markets where exhaust-emissions regulations require the fitment of catalytic converters, this includes control of exhaust gas recirculation, with the oxygen sensor in the exhaust up-stream of the three-way catalyst chamber.

Details of the V6 engine were released in July 1983, but the new ZX didn't appear until September. Then it was clear that whilst its greater power could give it a claim to be the fastest-ever Japanese production car, there had been little attempt to take advantage of its more compact dimensions. The shorter V6 did mean a lower bonnet line for the 300ZX, but it didn't bring a smaller, handier car. As Japan's first production V6 it is an engine of the future. Its first sporting application, good as it is in many ways, is a re-run of the recent past.

CHAPTER 8

The third generation

Enter the 300ZX

You can't blame a manufacturer for sticking to a successful formula. Millions have been spent on developing new models as diverse as the BMW 5-series, Renault 5 and Volkswagen Golf that, at a glance, are hard to distinguish from their predecessors. Purists might mourn the passing of the 'no frills' original Zs, but the elaborately equipped and more highly-priced 280ZX sold better than any of its forbears.

Once embarked upon, there isn't any turning back from a progressive move up-market. A new Silvia with a strong turbocharged four-cylinder engine could take the place of the original Z in the Nissan line-up — and British Z enthusiasts gave it a genuine welcome — but the ZX had to go onwards and upwards. It remained Nissan's sporting flagship and was to become the fastest and most expensive Japanese car available. With the 300ZX Nissan were aiming for the supercar class.

Their claim was based on power and performance. A 3-litre turbocharged engine is an extravagance by any standard and in the new and more aerodynamically-efficient ZX it promised a 155 mph maximum speed and 0-60 mph acceleration in less than 7 seconds — Jaguar and Porsche country, with a chance of giving a 3-litre Ferrari a run for its money. Reality, in the shape of independent tests of production cars, was not quite as impressive, though still enough to be much the fastest Z-car in either European or US specification. In Britain, *Autocar* achieved a timed 137 mph maximum, while *Motor* recorded 140.8 mph; corresponding 0-60 mph times were 7.2 and 6.8 seconds. A US version was reckoned to be good for 135 mph and 0-60 mph in about 7.3 seconds.

The figures, like the price, match the Porsche 944. Now, this was a new league for the Z-car and one which it entered with some trepidation. At a first price in the UK £4 under £17,000 in 1984, the 300ZX Turbo was over £4,000 more expensive than the Toyota Supra or Mitsubishi Starion Turbo and a higher price than either the Lotus Excel or the 944 (the Porsche's price overtook it a year later). The question then was whether or not it had the poise and refinement to live in this company. But we run ahead...

What, apart from the new V6 engine, makes a 300ZX? A completely new body for a start, which despite its similarities to the 280ZX does not share any outer panels. The dimensions are virtually identical; the wheelbase is the same and European versions — two-seater and 2+2 — are within fractions of an inch of the earlier car, while US versions are now the same length, which means 3 inches shorter than they were before.

In their publicity material Nissan make much of new design work carried out to give the ZX a fresh look, emphasizing 'driveability' (whatever that means in this context) and 'expressing a youthful look of dynamic power'. Study of the end result and the fifth-scale models on page 61 is illuminating. From it we see that 'Model A' from the 280ZX's styling process — which progressed to full-scale mock-up and was rejected at a late stage because of its rectangular headlamps — was resurrected five years later. There are differences, of course, especially in the headlamp and front bumper treatment, but it is hard to escape the view that the general shape was kept on the shelf to be brought out at 'facelift' time.

What it needed then was full aerodynamic development. By careful attention to detail, the more wedgy new shape was brought down to C_d 0.30, according to Nissan's own wind-tunnel figures. It is fair to point out that not everyone believed that such a dramatic improvement (from the 280ZX's 0.385) could come from relatively

Frontal aspect is what sets the 300ZX apart from its predecessor and contributes to major improvement in aerodynamics. The apron ahead of the bonnet and the bumper and spoiler assembly are flexible polyurethane. The bonnet scoop is exclusive to the Turbo model, also identified by copious badging, including moulded-in lettering on the offside of the air dam.

Headlamps are semi-retractable, thus meeting height regulations as well as aerodynamic requirements, yet also leaving lenses partly exposed at all times for daylight flashing. A simple system of links from an electric motor is designed to work even in the severest weather.

small changes. The windscreen angle has been increased by $1\frac{1}{2}$ degrees and the screen is now flush-mounted, while the door mirrors have been faired-in and there is partial concealment of lights and wipers.

The semi-retractable headlamps are perhaps the most striking styling feature of the 300ZX. With the more drooping nose that the new, shorter engine allowed, they undoubtedly make a major contribution to the improved aerodynamics. The idea is a good one for, unlike fully retractable lights, they can be used to flash a warning. The lamps retract 3 inches vertically by a simple system of levers connected to a step motor.

The whole front apron is flexible polyurethane, body colour above the bumper line, then shiny black for the bumper itself and the edge of the big air dam beneath it. A black spoiler is fitted to the trailing edge of the tailgate, while a similarly contrasting rubbing strip follows along the side of the car. To some, these look too much like aftermarket add-ons and spoil the clean line of the car. A version shorn of spoilers called 'SF' (for Sports Functional) impressed those who saw it in Japan at the time of the 300ZX launch, but has not been offered in Nissan's major export markets.

Z-car, 1985 style — in terms of complexity, sophistication, weight and price, the 300ZX Turbo is a far cry from the original 240Z of 1969. The progressive move up-market begun in the late 1970s has carried Nissan's sporting flagship to the brink of the supercar league, with a turbocharged 3-litre power unit and improved aerodynamics to supply the performance required in the market sector where it now finds itself.

The two-seater and 2+2 300ZXs are difficult to tell apart; only the extended rear quarter-window gives an outward clue. Only the 2+2 is sold in Britain, though both bodies are available elsewhere. The majority have the Targa T bar roof introduced on the 280ZX, with the same easily removed and installed smoked glass panels. Since there has been no more than a marginal increase in width inside the car, the same problem of luggage space and the spare wheel arises as in the UK-specified 280ZX. There is *just* room to stow the two roof panels in their vinyl pouches above the wheel and below the roller-blind luggage cover. The only solution to the luggage problem (with Dunlop's Denovo stopping production) is to treat the 2+2 as a two-seater and extend the load area by folding the

rear seats down. The brochure talks confidently of a wider boot which can accommodate two full-size golf bags, but that is strictly for markets that accept a 'mini-spare' which sits behind the trim at the side of the luggage compartment.

Under its new clothes the 300ZX has a mechanical layout much as before. Clearly there has been a good deal of development work in the suspension department to adapt the MacPherson-strut front end and semi-trailing-arm rear to the more exacting demands of 200 bhp-plus.

Efforts to cut down shock absorber friction and achieve close control of horizontal and vertical compliance of the strut bushes have paid dividends at the front. At the rear, firm front-rear and soft

Nissan, in common with other Japanese makers, have a good reputation for reliability. Extensive testing at the prototype stage is one reason for that. The 300ZX underwent complete climatic evaluation, including starting tests in the worst arctic conditions, simulated in the Nissan laboratories.

up-and-down compliance in the bushes improves cornering performance and straight-line stability without an adverse effect on the ride. Though the semi-trailing-arm rear suspension system is similar to the 280ZX, the springs and shock absorbers, previously concentric, are now separated in a layout shared with the latest Silvia coupe — the development of which, incidentally, fell to the same Nissan engineering group as the 300ZX.

Every suspension component has changed compared with the 280. At the front, castor was increased from 5 to 7 degrees and both trail and scrub radii decreased. Anti dive characteristics were also increased, as was anti-squat at the rear. The pivots of the semi-trailing arms are inclined inwards to promote negative camber through most of the suspension travel. The semi-trailing arms from the Silvia are inclined at 18 degrees to the wheel axis, instead of 23 degrees in the 280ZX, so there is less inherent camber change.

The effect of all this has been to give the 300ZX more precise handling and better steering feedback, but as with any high-performance car there has to be a trade-off between handling and ride quality. Reasoning that a comfortable ride is more important to most people when cruising around town and that sharp handling matters more than a soft ride when travelling at speed, Nissan offer the Turbo with adjustable shock absorbers, operated from a switch on the centre console. There are three positions, 'soft', 'normal' and 'firm', achieved by a small motor inside each damper housing which

The 2+2 is the only 300ZX body-style offered on the UK market, as is the Targa roof with its central T-bar and lift-out glass panels. There is something of an add-on look about the shiny black spoiler on the rear deck.

opens and closes an oil orifice.

Nissan were not the first to offer this device — which has similarities to the Armstrong Selectaride offered by Jensen and others in the 1960s — and although in theory it is a good idea, it isn't so impressive in practice. With 'soft' selected the ZX has a tendency to wallow while 'firm' gives a distinctly uncomfortable ride on anything other than a smooth road, so 'normal' is the best compromise for nearly all conditions... And that compromise, essentially what the engineers sought to optimize with the adjustable system, is still not as good as some of the 300ZX's rivals'.

Not that this is the easiest of problems to solve, given that the Turbo has some pretty massive and very low-profile tyres. The alloy

rims are 7 inches wide and wear 205/55 VR16 tyres at the front and 225/50 VR16 at the rear. The different widths are in the interest of handling balance, while it is said that the different profiles front and rear are to achieve the same rolling diameter. British-market Turbos are supplied on Japanese-made Dunlop SP Sport Super D4 or Bridgestone Potenza tyres. The non-turbo model has $6\frac{1}{2}$-inch rims (with four-stud fixing instead of the Turbo's five) with 210/60 VR390 Dunlop or Michelin TD tyres, which the car's handbook describes as 'run-flat', though the TD idea was intended mainly to ensure that the tyre stays on the rim in a blow-out rather than for extended running deflated. The Japanese SF specification has $5\frac{1}{2}$-inch steel wheels. Cars for the USA have the $6\frac{1}{2}$-inch alloy rims with 215/60 VR15 tyres all round, either Bridgestone, Toyo or Goodyear Eagle GT.

After the chopping and changing for the 280ZX variants, the 300 settled with rack-and-pinion steering with speed-related variable power assistance.With just 2.8 turns from lock to lock it is well geared for quick response.

The 300ZX brakes received attention, too, with larger ventilated discs at the front (11.8-inch Turbo, 10.8-inch non-Turbo) and plain discs at the rear (12.1-inch and 11.4-inch) with an 8-inch tandem servo. Tests showed that, at last, the ZX had effective and well-balanced brakes. The Bosch ABS anti-lock braking system also became available as an option in some markets.

While the 280ZX Turbo had been available *only* with automatic transmission when first announced, the 300ZX Turbo was only offered with a manual gearbox.This is the Borg-Warner five-speed, while the normally-aspirated car has Nissan's own. The non-turbo car has Nissan's E4N71B automatic transmission as an option. This has four speeds with a lock-up device for each. It also has two automatically selected modes, 'normal' and 'power', determining

A full-size spare wheel in cars sold in Britain means luggage space is severely restricted — as in the 280ZX — but the lift-up parcels shelf has been replaced by a roller blind installed in the crossbar. Folding down the seats to increase the luggage area requires the removal of this. Roof panels stow in vinyl pouches and (just) fit above the spare when the shelf is in place.

Interior layout is similar to the 280ZX, but quite different in detail. US-market cars are offered with electronic instrumentation, but UK keeps to a conventional dashboard. Key switches are at finger-tip reach either side of the instrument binnacle, and the new model is better provided with air outlets on the facia than its predecessor.

gearshifts and lock-up depending on the driving conditions (there is a manual override switch on the console). An automatic can be fitted to the Turbo, but it is a beefed-up version without the lock-up feature and with a manual switch-off for the overdrive top gear.

The driveline is otherwise as 280ZX. Final-drive ratio is 3.7:1 in the normally-aspirated car, 3.545:1 for the Turbo. Ratios in the Turbo's five-speed box are well chosen, with a long-legged (27.3 mph per 1,000 rpm) top which is just an overdrive — and in which maximum speed is achieved at about on the engine's power peak. The Turbo is fitted with a transmission oil cooler, to which the oil is diverted thermostatically when temperature exceeds 130 degrees C. Obviously there is some nervousness about transmission heat build-

up, as European models have a dashboard warning light marked 'Diff Oil'. The handbook suggests that, should it illuminate, the differential should be checked for leaks and if there are none the driver should slow down...

Inside, the 300ZX offers the whole range of gadgets from useful luxuries to pure gimmickry. The seat design is basically as the 280, but now the driver's seat has eight-way adjustment — either manual or power-operated. Three of the eight functions — lumbar, thigh and side supprt — are operated pneumatically, by a lever-operated inflater or an electric pump within the seat. A tiltable steering column with a 'memory' is available to make entry and exit easier for large people, as well as provide a further refinement of driving

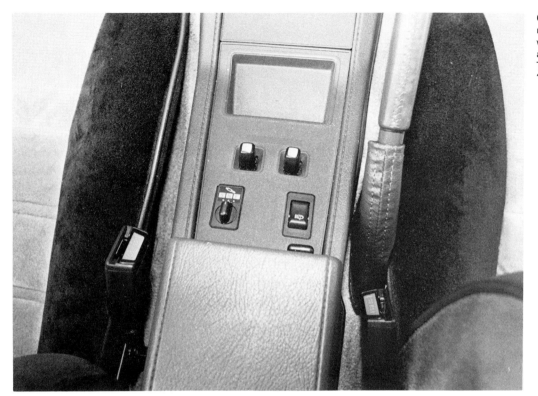

Centre console has two 'joysticks' for door mirror adjustment, switch for headlamp washers and — on Turbo models — adjustment for shock absorber stiffness. The rotary switch has three positions: 'soft', 'normal' and 'firm'.

position.

Equipment offered includes a cruise control, electric windows, electrically-adjustable door mirrors, air conditioning and an elaborate four-speaker stereo system but, strangely, no central locking.

British-market cars come with large, orange-on-black conventional instruments, but there is the inevitable electronic facia available in some other markets with a digital speedometer and bar-graph type rev-counter and supplementary instruments. With electronic facia the two central instrument spaces, otherwise filled by such useful instruments as oil pressure, voltmeter and turbo boost gauge, are used for an accelerometer and a compass.

Generally, the interior is better than the 280ZX, though there is still too much colour-coordinated leather-look plastic with phoney stitching for some tastes. And, though there is really no more room than before, the bigger glass area of the 300 gives a lighter, more airy feel.

Road & Track summed it up well by saying 'if you liked the 280, you'll love the 300ZX'. John Hartley, writing from Tokyo at the time of the new model's first showing, concluded that the 300ZX had 'the power but not the manners of a supercar'.

The chassis *is* competent, but it isn't a Porsche 944 or a Lotus in its balance or the subtle compromise between ride and handling. It is fast, though not raucously so. Though the Turbo has plenty of

This cutaway drawing of a US-specification 300ZX Turbo shows the key elements of the design, with turbocharged V6 engine set well back and revised suspension. Note that compared with the 280ZX (page 63) the rear springs and shock absorbers are separated in this new model. The semi-trailing-arm set-up is shared with the four-cylinder Silvia coupe.

power, 230 bhp is not remarkable for a boosted 3-litre and that relatively unstressed character shows in excellent flexibility. There is lag before the turbocharger comes into operation, but you hardly notice it because the engine pulls so strongly at the uncharged bottom end, below 2,000 rpm. In fact, it hardly feels like a turbo-car — until you look at the performance figures.

The 300ZX doesn't feel as heavy as its predecessor, but is actually substantially more weighty — a disappointment in view of the light new engine. Perhaps there is a lightweight, lithe fourth-generation Z somewhere in Nissan's future. *Autocar* observed: 'The Z-car continues to grow up; some say it has now reached middle age'. So have Nissan, for 1984 saw the company's 50th anniversary (Nissan Motor Company was set up in December 1933). It was celebrated in America with a special edition of the 300ZX in silver finish with flared wheelarches, 'ground effect' rocker panels, stiffer suspension and Pirelli P7 tyres on special gold-coloured wheels. The marriage of these 'supertyres' and the Z suspension is reportedly a slightly uneasy one, but just 5,000 cars were made and they had no trouble selling them.

That's the way it's been — especially in America — ever since the Z story started.

Not really a Z-car, but carrying the ZX name in the UK market — the four-cylinder Nissan Silvia Turbo found favour with those who bought the original Zs as a lighter, lower-priced car of somewhat similar character. The idea of using the Z's image to promote other Turbos in the Nissan range (the Cherry and Bluebird Turbos also have a ZX designation) was from Saatchi & Saatchi, Nissan UK's advertising agency.

US 50th Anniversary model celebrates the company rather than the Z's Jubilee — a 300ZX Turbo with special silver-and-black two-tone colour scheme, flared wheelarches to accommodate wide Pirelli P7 tyres and the leather upholstery-digital facia trim and equipment package; it was produced as a limited edition of 5,000 and sold at 26,000 dollars.

CHAPTER 9

Datsun-plus

Adding to the Z

A best-selling sports car was a natural for the accessory business, particularly in America, and a mini-industry has built up providing Z-car equipment. Some of the parts suppliers were in there from the start, as Datsun dealers loaded their hard-to-get 240Zs with extra goodies to command a premium price.

An owner survey by *Road & Track* in 1972 — less than two years after the car's launch — showed that no less than 38 per cent of the 106 owners polled had opted for, or had to accept, air conditioning and 24 per cent had alloy wheels and bigger-than-standard tyres. A few years later it was rare to see a Z without special wheels of some kind on either side of the Atlantic.

Since the trims for the standard wheels were the cars' worst feature aesthetically, the enthusiasm for alloy wheels is understandable. The 'slot mags' — simple aluminium alloy (not magnesium) wheels marketed in Britain by Wolfrace — were among the most popular and looked the part; 6-inch rims were regular wear, but some people were temped to go wider. However, even with superior tyres the improved grip is likely to be countered by extra harshness, or a lack of balance, and the already heavy steering becomes even more difficult to manage.

The other most frequent add-on modifications are spoilers and air dams. All but the very first UK cars came with a moulded rubber under-nose spoiler and a one-piece tail wing, but such items were not supplied as standard in the US, nor were they available as factory options there for some time. Brock Racing Enterprises, who ran the West Coast 240Z racing team, developed a useful sideline making parts for Datsuns. BRE's parts business eventually became Interpart, and one of their first products was the 'spook' (a cross between a spoiler and scoop) —

an air dam that, just like the factory item offered in Europe, had an improving effect on the car's stability. Today, while the Datsun Competition Parts Catalogue lists two kinds of front spoiler (rubber for pre-1975 models and glass-fibre for later types) and one-piece and three-piece rear ones, there are all shapes and sizes available from specialists throughout America and Europe. At their most extreme they are combined with a lengthened glass-fibre nose assembly (like the 'aerodyna' nose of the Japanese ZG competition cars) and/or a 'whale tail' like those allowed in IMSA GT racing.

There *is* a useful improvement in stability to be gained from the standard spoilers. When the Z was designed, such things were new, even for racing cars. In a styling sense the Z looks more 'pure' without them, but on a sports car with a macho image they became the thing to have, needed or not. The Z did, but on a standard car anything much bigger than those stock items is unlikely to boost much more than the owner's ego.

Also popular were the transparent headlamp covers that make the Z look like an early E-type Jaguar. Again, several kinds are available. The factory ones have chrome surrounds and look like those used by the works rally cars from time to time; others offer something similar with stainless-steel rims, while those made for the British Z-Club are plain with a thin rubber sealing ring. Two problems can result from such fitments — a loss of headlamp power and accuracy and condensation that not only cuts down the light, but can allow body rot to set in. Also, although American racing Zs have opaque glass-fibre lens covers, tests by the Competition Department has shown that this streamlining does not have a significant effect on the car's performance.

Early customizing — the 240Z became the Official Pace Car at the opening of Ontario Motor Speedway near Los Angeles. Finished in the paint style of the BRE racing Zs and with a big air dam, rear spoiler and special alloy wheels with oversize tyres, a whole series was made for a California dealer promotion — just like they do at Indianapolis.

A hard rubber chin spoiler, or air dam, was standard on all but the first few 240Zs sold in Britain, but remained an option in North America. This photograph shows the space for the sidelamp/indicator lens moulding that for legal reasons could not be used in Europe, where indicator units were repositioned above the bumper.

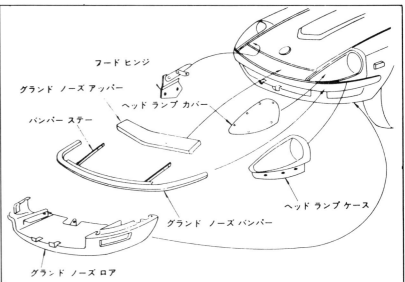

フード ヒンジ

グランド ノーズ アッパー

ヘッド ランプ カバー

バンパー ステー

ヘッド ランプ ケース

グランド ノーズ バンパー

グランド ノーズ ロア

The ultimate modification from the factory was to turn the Z into a ZG by fitting add-on wheelarch flares and the extended 'aerodyna' nose that closed off the top air intake, ZX-style. The diagram shows the additional glass-fibre parts needed and how they fit.

The rear deck spoiler extending over the bodywork on each side of the tailgate was also standard in the UK with badging attached, though the sticker tribute to a grand old racing driver who became very popular in the 1970s was a very special option!

While we are on the subject of Z customizing there is the ever-popular louvred rear window cover to which the car's almost flat tailgate glass is well suited. Some, like the Interpart LiftLouvre, fit neatly and securely over the glass and they do have the function of a sunshade as well as hiding items in the luggage compartment from prying eyes (a built-in 'parcels shelf' didn't come until the ZX). There is also that peculiarly American accessory, the 'bra', to protect the low nose from stone chips — the better ones, it is claimed, do not allow water trapped beneath the cover to cause more extensive body damage. . . .

But it isn't all down to appearances. With Z enthusiasm running so high, and the car's popularity for all kinds of motor sport, performance and handling improvements were inevitable. BRE were early in that market, too, making use of their racing experience to offer Mulholland shock absorbers (named after Mulholland Drive, behind Los Angeles — a twisty road used illegally by West Coast road racers to test their cars), springs and

Stylish sunshade — the louvred rear window cover should, if properly designed, hide objects in the luggage compartment, but not affect visibility through the rear-view mirror. This is the LiftLouvre, from Interpart, fitted to a 280Z; models are available for Zs and ZXs of all kinds and one type allows a rear window wiper to operate beneath it.

A range of plastic body parts made in England by Richard Grant Accessories fitted to a 260Z. The moulded front spoiler includes an air scoop and is extra-deep, while the strakes along the wing tops are inspired by BMW's racing CSL, but of doubtful practical value.

The 'bra' idea — a cover designed to protect the nose from stone chips and bad weather — started with American Porsche enthusiasts. Air-cooled cars are ideal for them, of course, but the smooth and vulnerable nose of the ZX also lends itself quite well to this tailormade cover by DaVest.

The ultimate in Z-car body-kits is this Ferrari GTO replica based on a first-series 240/260/280Z. Joe Alphabet, of Alpha Design, Huntington Beach, California, recognized the demand for rare and expensive GTOs and the similar overall dimensions of the Z. Front wings and bonnet are replaced by a glass-fibre moulding, Datsun doors and rear quarters skinned with Ferrari-shaped glass-fibre. In 1984 a conversion body kit cost 4,000 dollars; Alpha's rebuild, including Ferrari-like wire wheels and other trimmings, was about 14,500 dollars.

anti-roll bars. Bob Sharp Racing, associated with his Datsun dealership in Connecticut, put their continuing racing programme to good use in the development and sale of parts and accessories for Zs and ZXs; there is a wealth of experience there that goes back to the equipment they made for the 2000 Roadsters.

Today, because of emission control regulations, American engine tuning specialists have to state that their equipment is 'for off-road use only'. So the helpful people at Datsun Competition Department in Gardena cannot officially recommend any specifications for road cars, though they are always happy to advise on the right equipment for any competition application. Their extensive parts catalogue has a big section on Zs including all manner of exciting things. From it we learn that European-specification springs have 10 to 15 per cent more rate than those standard for the US and a 1-inch lower ride height and so, combined with solid rubber competition steering rack bushings,

they go some way to take the softness and vagueness out of later US Z-cars. A racing suspension system with adjustable ride height and gas-filled shock absorbers is also available, as is the factory rally suspension kit that *raises* the car by 1½ inches. Thicker anti-roll bars and a rear anti-roll bar kit for the pre-1974 models that did not have them are available. Brake modifications range from harder competition pads and linings for the standard set-up to FIA-approved four-piston calipers and a four-wheel disc brake kit that is an SCCA C-Production legal option.

A lot of specialists offer fabricated exhaust systems for the Z, but rather fewer have a range of camshafts and carburettor conversion kits. For a high-performance, but still well behaved road engine, the US Competition Department people would (if they were allowed to!) recommend a triple Mikuni-Solex carburettor set-up with small (34-mm) chokes, a 'slalom' (rally) cam and their twin-pipe exhaust system. Others fit triple Webers. Impact Parts, of Glen Wild, New York, offer a Holley four-barrel conversion which they claim is easy to instal, no problem to set up and, aside from offering 20 per cent more power and improved fuel economy, also eliminates the vapour lock, hesitation and

starting difficulties of 1973-4 US Z cars.

In Britain, most Z conversion work today is carried out by Fourways Engineering of Borough Green, Kent. They offer tailor-made engine and suspension mods for the Z variants and the ZX, with 160 bhp at the back wheels, a useful improvement without resorting to turbocharging. The best-known converted Z-cars are produced by Spike Anderson's company. 'Big Sam' was their race car, while the roadgoing cars were Super Samuris.

Some 70 two-seater and 2 + 2 Super Samuris have been made — the name applying to the 'full house' conversion with a distinctive two-tone orange-and-bronze paint job — but lots of other British Zs have some of Spike's equipment.

The first Super Samuri that formed the basis of subsequent conversions had a modified cylinder-head (of course), triple 40 DCOE Weber carburettors, a six-branch exhaust, lowered suspension with Koni shock absorbers and wider Midland Metallic alloy wheels. It also had AP four-piston front brake calipers fitted after the original equipment proved inadequate for the extra performance. With a 9.5:1 compression ratio and a standard camshaft this set-up gave about 185 bhp and

An early Samuri conversion on a 240Z carrying the name of Spike Anderson's Race Head Services company. Later cars were wilder, but carried through the same orange-and-bronze paint job.

independent tests showed a 0-60 mph time of 6.4 seconds and 0-100 mph in 17 seconds. The original car (registered FFA 169L) had quite a history. It did a variety of club motor sport events before being bought back by Anderson after 80,000 miles. He then fitted a more potent racing engine, with triple Dellorto carburettors and a wilder cam — it was reputed to give 217 bhp — and put it back on the road.

The other regular Datsun fettler is Janspeed Engineering, in Salisbury, who offer a range of equipment for the Z among their bewildering selection of conversions and tuning aids. They were among the first to offer a turbocharged conversion for the Z, and ready-converted 260Zs were sold by Datsun (Bristol) Ltd in 1979 for around £7,000 — £1,400 more than a 260Z two-seater at the time. The 260Z Turbo used Janspeed's already well-tried bolt-on turbo kit, with a Rotomaster turbocharger sucking air through a 2-inch SU carburettor. Compression ratio on this car was unchanged and so the boost was limited to a modest 5 psi. Other modifications were few — an oil cooler and some harder brake pads and 'Turbo' sidewinder stripes.

Performance was impressive and with the standard compression ratio the transition from uncharged to charged was much less marked than with many turbo conversions. 0-60 mph in 6.6 seconds and a standing quarter-mile in 15.3 seconds were effortlessly achievable and a tremendous improvement over the standard European-specification 260Z.

Soon after the ZX appeared, Janspeed developed a turbo conversion. It was a more difficult job than the 260Z for although fuel-injection is theoretically well suited to matching with a turbocharger, the Bosch electronic system of the ZX is tricky to adapt to the fuel demands of a 7-psi air intake boost. Janspeed's solution is ingenious — they fit two extra cold-start injectors close to the throttle, triggered by higher-than-atmospheric pressure in the inlet manifold, and these produce extra fuel for the boosted phase. Again, few other modifications were deemed necessary. The result was about 30 per cent increase in power and torque, 2.5 seconds off the standard car's 0-60 mph acceleration time (7.3 seconds for the turbo) and 11 seconds quicker to 100 mph. *Autocar* tested the Janspeed two-seater in 1980 and were impressed — though not by the brakes, which showed that harder pad material is needed if stopping is to match the extra speed of a

Acceleration tests with the Janspeed Turbo 260Z carried out by *Autocar* Note the car's ride height near its maximum speed — rare photographic proof of how aerodynamic lift can affect a car.

The Janspeed turbo conversion of the 260Z is simple, using a Rotomaster turbocharger to draw air through a single 2-inch SU carburettor — all of which fit neatly alongside the engine.

Adapting a turbocharger to the fuel-injected L28E engine proved quite a complex problem for Janspeed. The electronics of the injection system are set up for the normally aspirated engine and need to be 'tricked' by extra injectors to provide enough fuel in the boosted phase. In 1980, when the conversion was first developed, it cost £782 plus fitting.

modified ZX.

Nissan's own Turbo ZX came to America in 1981, but in the US a number of firms had long offered turbocharger kits. One firm, Car Tech, of Dallas, Texas, specialized in Z turbo conversions, but credit for the most highly developed Z cars must go to Scarab, in San Jose, California. Their President, Brian Morrow, describes Scarab's work as ' a new concept in automobile remanufacturing'. They bring new life to old Z cars — by fitting Chevrolet V8 engines.

A Scarab is a complete Z rebuild, starting with 'a selected, previously owned (secondhand!) bodyshell'. Mostly the cars are supplied complete from the company, but they also offer a do-it-yourself conversion kit (you supply the Z and engine and gearbox) which can be applied to anything from a 240Z to a 280ZX and is

bolt-on, the installation being possible without any cutting or sheet-metal bending.

The original 240Z-based Scarabs used the 327-cu-in (5.3-litre) small-block Chevy V8, balanced and blueprinted and developing 250 bhp. It was mated to a Borg-Warner T10 four-speed gearbox with a Hurst shifter. Koni adjustable shock absorbers were specified, along with heavier anti-roll bars, Teflon bushings in the front compression struts and stiffer steering-rack mounts. Tyres: 195/70 front, 250/70 rear, Pirelli CN36 or P7. Four-piston front brakes were also recommended.

The result of this surprisingly neat installation — the V-8 fits snugly into the Z's generous engine bay — is a car that is fast, very

The Scarab is a latter-day AC Cobra with a Chevrolet V8 engine in place of the Nissan six. 'Full house' versions have a number of cosmetic changes inside and out, like the BBS wheels on this example. Scarab have supplied 250 complete cars and over 4,000 V8 conversion kits.

A Chevrolet V-8 engine fits snugly into the Z engine bay, complete in this case, with an air-conditioning pump. The pancake carburettor air cleaner has been removed for this photograph.

flexible (maximum torque of the 327 is 360 lb ft at 3,600 rpm) and untemperamental. Performance raches into the supercar class — Scarab's own figures suggest 0-60 mph in 5.6 seconds and a 13.2-second standing quarter-mile. Later cars have used the 350-cu-in (5.7-litre) Chevrolet V-8 and Scarab now offer a range of newly built-up engines developing from 300 bhp to a turbocharged unit with 425 bhp.

Scarab started to produce ZX-based cars in 1981 and they have also built some automatics. A complete Scarab is luxuriously trimmed, with leather door panels, deep pile carpets and Recaro seats, and exterior changes can range from a TransAm front spoiler with integral brake ducts to a big three-piece rear wing, flared wheelarches and louvred bonnet vents. Some cars have rectangular headlamps, a feature shared with recent bodywork kits offered by Jim Cook Racing, of Los Alamitos, California, and Dave Kent's Creative Car Craft, of Hawthorne, near Los Angeles, who did bodywork for many racing and special Zs in the early days.

There is almost nothing — sensible, legal or otherwise — that you can't do to a Z-car, although it is surprising, perhaps, that

more people haven't made convertibles. There have been a couple of attempts in the US and of course there are any number of sunroofs available, but chopping the complete roof off a Z isn't something to be undertaken lightly. The factory knew that — and were only prepared to go as far as the T-bar for the ZX.

Impact Parts
Glen Wild Road
Glen Wild
New York 12738

CarTech Manufacturing
11144 Ables Lane
Dallas
Texas 75229

Jim Cook Racing
PO Box 173

Los Alamitos
California 90720

Creative Car Craft
3944 W El Segundo Boulevard
Hawthorne
California 90250

Da-Vest Inc
3220 W 71st Avenue
Westminster
Colorado 80030

Useful addresses in USA

Nissan Competition Department
PO Box 191
Gardena
California 90247

Bob Sharp Racing Parts &
Accessories Inc
021 South Street
Danbury
Connecticut 06810

Scarab Automobiles
PO Box 9217
San Jose
California 95157

Interpart
PO Box 390
Gardena
California 90247

Useful addresses in UK

Nissan UK Ltd
Nissan House
Columbia Drive
Worthing
West Sussex
BN13 3HD

Janspeed Engineering Ltd
Castle Road
Salisbury
Wiltshire SP1 3SQ

Fourways Engineering Company
Performance Car Centre
10-12 Maidstone Road
Borough Green
Kent

Spike Anderson Cylinder Heads
Unit 7
Silverstone Circuit
Silverstone
Northants

CHAPTER 10

Production racer

Track successes

Datsun's involvement in racing in America started some years before the Z-car. The 510 Bluebird saloon, introduced in 1967, quickly gained a good reputation as a low-priced competition car, while the three generations of Fairlady Roadsters were already popular in SCCA racing.

One amateur racer with a 1600 Roadster was Dick Roberts. In the mid-1960s he travelled all over the United States to Sports Car Club of America meetings. He was still doing so in 1985, though now in the capacity of Nissan Competition Manager. The Competition Department was set up at Nissan's US headquarters in Gardena, California, in 1967. Rather than enter cars on their own account, the department co-ordinates the activities of independent teams on contract, develops parts with them, and sells the results to the large number of privateers using Nissan cars.

At the time of the 240Z's arrival, the two main Datsun protagonists were Bob Sharp and Pete Brock. Sharp, from Connecticut, scored Datsun's first racing wins in America and won the make's first SCCA National Championship — F-Production in 1967. Brock's BRE team made them regular winners, and started a 10-year run of success for the Z-car in the C-Production category.

BRE's efforts were an important part of Datsun's image-building for the 240Z. An amateur racer, Brock was Carroll Shelby's first employee in the AC Cobra days and the designer of the Cobra Daytona coupe. He first became involved with Datsun almost out of spite. He had set up Brock Racing Enterprises as a sideline when working for Shelby and prepared a couple of racing saloons for Hino Motors. There weren't many rules for racing small saloons in America at that time and Brock was able to build two 'cheater' cars for a not very serious supporting race at the 1966 *Times* Grand Prix at Riverside — forerunner of the CanAm. The two little Hinos ran away with the race. Unbeknown to Brock, the race was watched by senior management from the big Japanese manufacturers, Datsun and Toyota, both of which were beginning their big sales push into the United States and had seen the high degree of American manufacturer involvement in racing. Little-league Hino, better known for their trucks and buses than their cars, had beaten the big names at Riverside. Afterwards, BRE had approaches from both Nissan and Toyota to run racing programmes for them. . . .

Brock, who was soon to be running BRE full-time, decided to stay with Hino and was even building a racing GT prototype, the Samurai, using their components. Then Hino found itself resisting a takeover bid by Toyota and Brock, caught in the cross-fire, was offered the new Toyota US motor sports programme to run. But his old boss Shelby, who had a Toyota dealership, out-manoeuvred him and got the contract instead. BRE were set up to go racing, but had no cars, so Brock approached Nissan. The people in Los Angeles didn't want to play, so he used his connections in Japan and eventually was given cars and finance to run a team of 2000 Roadsters by the factory. It was 1968, a good time for SCCA sports car racing. BRE's two Datsuns lined up against Shelby's Toyota 2000 GTs, two Triumph TRs from Kas Kastner and Porsche 914/6s run by Richie Ginther. The Datsuns did well, the link was consolidated and, though the relationship with the US Nissan headquarters remained cool, the next year's programme was brought under their wing.

Dominant Datsun — the BRE 240Z that John Morton drove to victory in the SCCA C-Production category two years in a row. This West Coast team run by Pete Brock set the standards for production car racing at the time and started a 10-year run of championship success for the Z-car.

BRE had started racing with Datsun before the Z-car and continued with a 510 saloon programme alongside the Z. Morton's Bluebird in the TransAm Challenge had a family identity with the 240Z — even to the race number.

Towards the end of a second successful year with the Roadsters, the factory took Brock into their confidence about future plans. He remembers: 'They showed me the pictures of the Z-car and I was flabbergasted because at that time it was just the most beautiful car I'd ever seen. I said: "Is this a dream car?" and they said: 'No, it's a production car for next year''. They told me all the specifications and I went home on a cloud. I went back to the guys in the shop and said you are not going to believe what I'm going to tell you, but it's just Christmas — next year we've got the most incredible car you can imagine.'

BRE had the second 240Z to arrive in the States, a few weeks before the car's October 1969 introduction. The team had gained a reputation for the best race preparation on the West Coast and apart from having good people on the mechanical side, Brock's design background insisted that they always look good, with smart red-and-white livery and a concours finish.

The six-cylinder engines were new to them and the first thing they ran into when preparing the Z was a major vibration problem. 'We were soon getting some real horsepower, but it was vibrating so bad it would nearly shake itself off the dyno,' says Brock. Though this information was sent back to Japan they got no feedback and so they looked around for other six-cylinder engines that might have the same problem. Jaguar was the obvious one and BRE fitted a harmonic balancer from the E-type. It worked — up to a point. Japan were working on a solution, but the first race for the Z would have to be run without the revised crankshafts. 'So we had to red-line the engine below the harmonic problem', Brock recalls. 'Even so, at that first race, at Riverside, the cars ran off and hid. But the vibration got so bad that it shook the clutches apart and we didn't finish. But the writing was on the wall.'

The same problem meant that sixth was the best they could do in the second outing, but shortly afterwards the clutches were rigged so that even if the springs locating the pressure plate vibrated away they would keep in engagement and keep going. It was enough for the BRE 240Z to score its first win. Their engine man, Art Oehrli, welded counterweights to the standard crank and achieved an improvement, but such modifications were not allowed under SCCA rules. Then the factory produced some new crankshafts. Technically they were illegal, too, at that time

Bob Sharp was one of the most consistently successful Z-racers. His first 240Z C-Production car eventually became a 280Z and passed to Jim Fitzgerald, who extended its racing career to a full decade. The car that entered 120 races and 'won too often to count' started as a show vehicle, but went to Sharp's racing shop in Connecticut after an over-enthusiastic photographic model made a dent in the roof!

because they weren't the same as those in the production cars so avidly awaited by the Z's first US customers. But they had been put into line production back in Japan and would come through in due course. BRE ran three or four events in this 'grey area', unsure if the scrutineers would ban them if they called for an engine strip and very worried that Nissan might 'lose face' if they were accused of cheating.

'When we got the proper cranks we could really make them run', Brock remembers. Oehrli's development gave them 265 bhp early on, 280-285 bhp regularly, and a usable 305 bhp by the time the team was disbanded in 1972.

All of this came as something of a surprise to the Japanese engineers. Their High Performance Department concentrated on purpose-built race engines, like the Prince-derived S20 twin-cam 24-valve 2-litre that powered the Z432 model. But this could not be used in SCCA as the model was not on sale in the USA. The idea of running the production single-cam to very high rpm was new to them but, according to Brock, their attitude changed when BRE sent them a full race L24 engine which would rev to 8,000 and produce 280 horsepower! The S20 was only giving around 210 bhp and it is said that the Japanese ran the BRE L24 and were amazed to find it was reliable and would blow off everything else in their domestic racing scene. Suddenly communication between Japan and the US picked up!

BRE's agreement with Nissan — and that of Bob Sharp Racing, on the East Coast — was for a full interchange of information. This attitude of sportsmanship was encouraged in particular by Yutaka Katayama, the President of Nissan US, a tremendous racing enthusiast, and the impetus behind the competitions promotion.

John Morton, in a BRE 240Z, won the SCCA C-Production National Championship two years in a row in 1970 and 1971. The team ran 510 saloons in the TransAm series and took two years of class wins there, finishing first and second in nine events out of ten in 1972. The BRE Zs had been sold to Logan Blackburn and Don Parkinson after the 1971 season. The street cars were selling well and Nissan reckoned that the initial promotion had worked; they transferred their efforts to creating a new image for the 1600 Sedan.

Looking back, Brock doesn't reckon that Nissan USA have capitalized on their racing since those days as well as they might.

Toyota overtook them in sales and although they have done virtually no racing since the unsuccessful 2000GT sortie, their more sporting cars have managed to achieve a similar kind of image to the Z today.

Be that as it may, there is no doubt that numerically there are more Datsuns racing in America than any other make. Dick Roberts estimates that there are some 800 active Datsun racers. of whom maybe 250 have Z-cars, and that the total is in thousands if you include those who take part in local rallies, autocross and gymkhanas. He claims that Nissan USA have the largest competition parts operation in the world, with a turnover of 4½ million dollars a year. (Some of the items they offer were covered in Chapter 9).

It is clear that Roberts and Brock didn't get along. Brock wanted a long-term contract that wasn't forthcoming, and after a brief flirtation with Formula 5000 he pulled out of racing at the end of 1973 and built up a new business making hang-gliders.

Change-over time. Jim Fitzgerald's new 280ZX and Frank Leary's 280Z together at the SCCA National Championship run-offs at Road Atlanta, in October 1979. In the background, Leary, 1978 C-Production Champion, talks to Z enthusiast and occasional works driver Sam Posey.

The main 'official' Z teams since have been Bob Sharp Racing (Sharp himself has won three C-Production National titles since 1972 as well as Sedan championships) and Electramotive, run by John Knepp and Don Devendorf on the West Coast. Before the 300ZX, top SCCA racing Z-cars were all turned into 280Zs — or ZXs — with the biggest permitted L28 engine and three Solex-Mikuni carburettors replacing the fuel-injection; 300 to 305 bhp is the 'standard' racing output with the right pistons, cam and manifolds, but some claim up to 340 bhp.

Some of the Zs racing in SCCA have been going for years. Jim Fitzgerald's 280Z C-Production car was a good example. It was finally put out to grass at the end of 1979 when Fitzgerald adopted a new 280ZX. His original Z-car had been the sixth 240Z to appear in the US. It started as the pride of Nissan's show fleet, but a lady model made an unexpected dent in its roof when posing for publicity shots and it was shipped to Bob Sharp Racing to be convered into a race car. This machine has a string of race wins to its credit and Fitzgerald eventually acquired it from Sharp to extend its racing career beyond anything that had been dreamed of nine years before. Outwardly it was a regular up-to-date Z-racer with flared wheelarches and a ground-scraping front air dam proudly proclaiming 'Datsun'. Underneath it had progressed from 240 to 260 and 280Z. Even by SCCA standards, where a Datsun 1600 Roadster could still win a National Championship in 1982, Fitzgerald's Z had a good run.

Z-cars dominated the C-Production category for 10 years. Morton and Sharp took two championship wins apiece in 1970-1 and 1972-3, respectively, Walt Maas' 260Z won in 1974, Bob Sharp was back in the winner's circle with a 280Z in 1975, and then it was Elliot Forbes-Robinson (1976), Logan Blackburn (1977), Frank Leary (1978) and in 1979, first year of the ZX, one P. L. Newman.

PLN is better known as Paul Newman, film actor, superstar and though now in his 60s, a remarkably good racing driver. A late starter in the sport — his interest was aroused by making the film *Winning* — he won his first National Championship in 1976 with a Triumph TR6 after an epic dice with Lee Mueller's works TR7. He subsequently became a regular winner in Bob Sharp's Datsun team, sponsored by Budweiser beer.

The first four ZXs in SCCA racing were for Newman, Jim Fitzgerald, Logan Blackburn and Bob Leitzinger. Newman's 280ZX made its debut at Summit Point Raceway in May 1979 and took pole position. On a wet and muddy track on race day he led from the start, dropped back to find his way through the puddles and neatly took back the lead by a comfortable 14 seconds. It was a good start for the new model which Sharp's chief mechanic Gene Crowe described as 'like building a completely new car' because of its different suspension design from the Z. Newman went on to win six out of eight races to become North East Divisional Champion and beat Blackburn and Leitzinger in the National Championship run-offs at Road Atlanta.

Since the mid-1970s Datsun have also been well represented in the increasingly important International Motor Sports Association racing series. There they have run in the GTU class for under-2½-litre cars. Since there has not been a 240Z since 1974 you may wonder why this is allowed, but IMSA, like Bill France's NASCAR racing, is more concerned with getting a closely competitive field than the niceties of homologation. GTU Z-cars run with a 2,486-cc version of the six-cylinder engine.

PLN in action in the first ZX racer — the Bob Sharp Racing machine sponsored by Canon cameras, Pioneer car stereo and Budweiser beer. The Datsun 'We are driven' slogan on the rear quarters undersells the degree of Nissan involvement.

Specialists in this category are the Electramotive team, based at El Segundo, near Los Angeles. Run by John Knepp, an engineer who used to work for Pete Brock's BRE team, and driver Don Devendorf, they started to enter a Z in the IMSA series in 1978, having supplied the engines and drive-trains for the car with which Brad Frisselle had won the GTU class in 1976. Devendorf scored one win in 1978, but the team's real success came the following season with their new ZX that won first time out in the demanding six-hour race at Riverside and went on to give Devendorf and Datsun championship victories with nine wins out of 13 races.

Bob Sharp Racing went into GTU with Paul Newman in 1980. Sam Posey, runner-up in a Z in 1977, had scored some IMSA successes for the team in 1979, including an excellent win from the back of the field at Lime Rock. Newman's record in 1980 shows a couple of second places, but it turned out to be the year of the Wankel, with the rotary-powered Mazda RX7s dominating the class. They could produce 300 bhp in IMSA form while the best that a 2.5-litre Datsun could muster while staying within the rules was 270 bhp.

Championship trio. P L Newman, racing driver and film star, won C-Production at Road Atlanta in 1979 from fellow Datsun ZX drivers Logan Blackburn (left) and Bob Leitzinger (right).

The IMSA ZX V8 Turbo prepared by the Bob Sharp team had little Datsun ZX left in it. The drooping nose and squared-off tail concealed tubular chassis frames and only the centre cockpit section, still production-based, was recognizable from the original car.

Devendorf had some pretty strong things to say about the equivalence formula for Wankels and piston engines, but clearly Datsun had to move on. Turbocharging gave them the chance. The new ZX Turbo road car was due for announcement in spring 1981. They could move out of the GTU category and into IMSA

The IMSA ZX V8 Turbo photographed at an early test session to show the tubular chassis frame at the front that carries the Nissan President engine and modified MacPherson strut suspension.

GTO. A 2.8-litre turbo had the potential of 500 to 550 bhp. Electramotive, Bob Sharp and Fred Stiff got to work developing the new model, canting the engine over at 45 degrees towards the passenger side, a dodge allowed by the regulations that would permit better cooling and more efficient plumbing for the turbocharger.

But, for a couple of seasons this Turbo ZX was to be overshadowed by another, more exciting project. Although 500 horsepower was enough to come to terms with the Porsche 934, the 924 Turbo and the less developed BMW M1s, to compete with the Porsche 935s that dominated IMSA's premier class more like 700 bhp was needed. Bob Sharp had a plan.

'We didn't like playing second-fiddle at IMSA races,' said Sharp. 'We wanted to run with the big cars.' But to do that they need a bigger engine and that engine had to come from a production car of the same make. Datsun didn't have a bigger engine. Or did they? In Japan, there was a limited-production limousine called the Nissan President, with a 4½-litre engine that looked for all the world like a classic American pushrod V8. At one time there had been some thoughts of using it in an Indianapolis car. With two turbochargers and 4.2-litres capacity it would be at the limit of the regulations and ought to produce a comfortable 700 bhp.

Sharp had first put his idea to Dick Roberts in 1977, but Nissan vetoed it as they only wanted to race what they sold and at that time a turbocharged production car wasn't even in prospect. Undaunted, Sharp obtained an engine from an unused President that had been brought to the United States but could not be registered because it did not meet Federal regulations. Gene Crowe, who had worked on the Cro-Sal McKee Oldsmobile and Commander McLaren-Chevrolet turbo CanAm cars, got to work. When Roberts learned of the Turbo road car in 1979 he was able to give Sharp's racer the go-ahead. It would provide a logical next step for his sponsor-attracting driver Paul Newman.

If the car was to be allowed to race it would have to run in IMSA's new 'All American GT' category. Since both the silhouette and the power unit started life in Japan that might have been a problem but, as we have seen, IMSA's rules are made to be 'adjusted' and with the prospect of a car — any car — that could challenge a run of Porsche victories that had become boringly predictable, IMSA's director John Bishop agreed that this American project could qualify.

The rules said that it had to keep the original car's wheelbase and maintain the essential elements of the ZX's body shape. While Crowe developed the engine, using Lucas fuel-injection and a pair of Roto-Master turbochargers, Trevor Harris, who had worked with Shadow and also designed the Frissbee CanAm car, designed a new racing chassis in which a multi-tube frame connected to part of the centre-section of the ZX monocoque. The big 4,150-cc engine was mounted well back and a CanAm-type Hewland LG transaxle in unit with the clutch was installed at the rear. Surprisingly, but mostly because of the under-bonnet space needed for the turbos, MacPherson strut-type suspension was retained at the front; in fact, the set-up is exactly as used on the BMW 320 Turbo race car. Rear suspension is by unequal-length wishbones and coil springs and Lola single-seater suspension uprights are used. Brakes are massive 13-inch vented discs, ATE at the front, Lockheed inboard at the rear. The wheels are Ronal, 16-inch diameter and 12-inch wide at the front; 19-inch diameter and 16.5-inch wide at the rear. Power steering was needed and was adapted from a Ford Mustang system.

Testing at Daytona at the end of 1980 showed a top speed on

Electramotive's IMSA GTO 208ZX Turbo came good for the 1982 season when Don Devendorf scored six category wins in 10 races. Devendorf teamed up with Tony Adamowicz (they were to become regular partners in IMSA endurance races) to drive the Electramotive ZX Turbo in an international event at Fuji in Japan.

The 300ZX shape and Nissan's new V6 engine provided Paul Newman's contender for the 1984 TransAm series, but it wasn't an instant success for the Bob Sharp team. Newman's running mate Jim Fitzgerald won the amateur GT-1 category with a similar car.

the banked circuit of 208 mph. The Twin Turbo ZX raced for the first time at Elkhart Lake in September 1980, though it had only had a couple of test days before then. The engine broke.

It was never to be a great success. IMSA racing was changing; racing prototypes were allowed in the top GTX class. The 911-derived Porsches gave way to Lola and March sports-racers. The Sharp Twin Turbo ZX was too heavy and made too many compromises to succeed in this company. At the end of 1981 the project was abandoned.

Meanwhile, in the GTO class, Don Devendorf had overcome initial difficulties and gone on to capture the 1982 Championship with six wins in the 'Little Turbo' 280ZX. 1983 was to bring problems again in the first half of the season — trifling things mainly, but they kept Electramotive out of the results — until Brainerd, Minnesota, in July, where Devendorf and Tony Adamowicz scored the first of four consecutive GTO class wins. At Road America, Wisconsin, they very nearly won the race outright, finishing second to the works GTP Ford Mustang in a 500-mile race stopped prematurely because of torrential rain.

The little track at Brainerd assumed a major significance for

Nissan as, one year before the 1983 return to IMSA form, Bob Sharp and Paul Newman decided to try their chances in the SCCA Professional TransAm race in Minnesota as a test for a possible programme in 1983. Driving his regular SCCA 'amateur' GT-1 280ZX Turbo — 2.5-litre engine — with only the GT-1 inlet restrictor removed, Newman led from start to finish.

Not surprisingly, Sharp decided to go TransAm for 1983. A more specialized car was built with a tube-frame chassis from Ron Nash Engineering, a 2.6-litre engine with Bosch fuel injection and the bigger wheels and brakes that the Professional series allowed. The results did not follow the Brainerd promise. Newman had a poor season, with a couple of third places his best results in TransAm, though he did win some races in GT-1.

With the 300ZX's arrival in 1984, Bob Sharp's team set to preparing a new TransAm car with the V6 engine at its maximum allowed capacity of 2.8 litres installed in a similar tube-frame chassis with a five-speed Weismann transmission. A series of retirements and a couple of fourth places were all that Newman had to show for his 1984 TransAm season, but veteran Jim Fitzgerald was able to use a broadly similar car to capture the national GT-1

The Nissan GTP ZX-Turbo is an out-and-out racer built on a Lola chassis and with a Nissan ZX Turbo V6 engine amidships. Aerodynamic development was carried out at the Imperial College wind-tunnel in London and by the Electramotive team in California, who are responsible for the IMSA racing project on behalf of Nissan USA.

title. A 280ZX driven by Morris Clement took the 1984 SCCA GT-2 Championship at the run-offs at Road Atlanta.

While the re-organization of the SCCA categories was giving the Zs another chance, in IMSA it again became clear that something more special than a production-based chassis was needed to make an impact. Electramotive reckoned that the 300ZX's VG30 V6 had the potential to power a fully-fledged GTP prototype that could take on the Porsche 962s, Jaguar XJR-5s and other prototypes in IMSA's top rank. Nissan USA agreed to underwrite the construction of a mid-engined GTP car based on a Lola T810. An aluminium honeycomb/carbon-fibre chassis was used with an Electramotive-prepared engine producing some 650 bhp at 8,000 rpm. Design work started in July 1984. The Nissan GTP ZX Turbo ran for the first time at Riverside in April 1985 and finished 11th at Laguna Seca a week later.

With the Japanese manufacturers providing engines for everything from Formula 1 (Honda) to Group C endurance racing (Toyota and Mazda) this policy of putting the Nissan name to a specialized racing chassis using their engine seems a likely course for the future.

Showroom Stock categories for virtually standard road cars have produced some spectacular racing and useful results for Z cars, starting with Dale Fazekas' wins in 1977 and 1978 and continuing more recently with the efforts of Izzy and Luis Sanchez, shown here driving 300ZX and 280ZX respectively.

Night-time at Le Mans in 1975, and the 260Z entered by Hans Schuller spends much of its time up on blocks in the pits having the differential repaired. The car was an ex-factory rally machine — compare the registration number with the 1974 RAC Rally entry illustrated in the next chapter.

The Z continued to have a competition career in Britain well into the 1980s. The immaculate 240Z prepared by Fourways Engineering for John Istead won both the BARC and ACSMC sprint championships in 1981, achieving 15 wins from 17 events on racing circuits and hill-climbs. Istead's 1972 car is fully road-equipped and was driven to all the events.

Production racing in Europe — this 260Z 2+2 qualified as a saloon car for the Spa 24 Hour race in 1975 and was modified to the 'Francorchamps' rules. Driven by Belgians Delbar, Rubens and Miroux, it ran as high as 10th, but failed to finish.

Back to standard

There is still an enthusiastic following for racing cars that are nearer to standard. The SCCA introduced a Showroom Stock class in 1977 for cars in 'as delivered' specification including complete road equipment — bumpers, silencers and all — with only safety modifications permitted. Winner of the Showroom Stock A category for the first two years was Dale Fazekas in a 280Z, but then the Saab Turbos took over. Datsun returned with a Showroom Stock winner in 1982 — a 280ZX driven by Luiz Sanchez. His brother Izzy used a 280ZX Turbo to win the newly introduced Showroom Stock GT category in 1983, while Larry Hendricks carried on the normally aspirated car's winning ways in SSA.

Ten years before, there had been talk of the 260Z 2+2 competing in Group 1 Production Saloon Car racing in Britain when it was discovered that its interior dimensions were such that it would qualify as a saloon rather than a GT car. In fact, no such entry was made, nor did the two-seater appear in the newly introduced Group 3 'Prodsports' races at club meetings.

At an international level, Group 3 did not have a great following, though a British entrant, London-based estate agent

First home win for the Z was at Suzuka in 1970. By 1972 the long-nose 240ZG was the most successful in Japan and in this wet race at the Mount Fuji circuit, Haruhito Yanagida scored a victory over a gaggle of modified Zs.

Martin Birrane, campaigned his ex-rally 240Z all over Europe in 1972 and even had an entry in the Le Mans 24 Hours, though he failed to qualify.

The only Z actually to race at Le Mans was the German entry of Hans Schuller, in 1975, which was also the first Japanese car to compete in this most famous of endurance events; it finished 26th. A 260Z 2 + 2 did take part as a saloon in the Spa-Francorchamps 24 Hours Touring Car race in 1975.

What seems to have been the first track championship success for the Z outside America and Japan went to a British firm called the Samuri Motor Company, who specialized in performance conversions for Z-cars. Their 240Z 'Big Sam', driven by Win Percy (who was later to become British Saloon Car Champion at the wheel of a Mazda RX7) beat a couple of quick Porsche Carreras to win the 1974 BARC Modsports Championship in 1974. 'Big Sam' was modified to Group 4 regulations and it subsequently appeared in a number of international sports car events in Britain.

What of the Z's competition career back home in Japan? Its first appearances there at the Fuji and Suzuka circuits were early in 1970 with the 24-valve Z432 model which in its first season was more often than not beaten by the SR311 Roadster. The 1970 All-Japan Suzuka 1,000 Kms goes down as the Z's first outright win in Japan, but thereafter the record is not as impressive as one might have thought, mainly because the cars usually competed with out-and-out racing machinery. The 240Z appeared in production events in 1971, and by 1972 the 240ZG, with its 'aerodyna' nose, became the regular racing machine, displacing the Z432. The American experience had shown that the production engine, with its single camshaft and two valves per cylinder was capable of a greater power output than the special dohc racing engine, which was restricted to 2-litres: 'there's no substitute for cubic inches' was proved again.

The 260ZG first appeared at the end of 1974 and, as in America, the racing cars kept pace with the engine enlargement of the road car, becoming a 280ZG in 1976.

A privateer, Haruhito Yanagida, who had raced Datsuns for several years, had a particularly successful season in 1978 when the rotary Mazdas formed strong opposition. Like some other Japanese private entrants he took his cars abroad for some events in the Far East.

Though it is not strictly racing, and in fact does not fit properly anywhere in the model's competition history, it should be recorded that the Z broke some speed records over the years. In 1972, camshaft specialist 'Racer' Brown did 152.134 mph at Bonneville Salt Flats in a 240Z and reckoned that with more power and further modifications a Z would do 165 mph. Tom O'Connor, who worked for the Datsun Competition Department, went to Bonneville in 1975 with a 280Z and proved him nearly right. Using the usual speed record streamlining including smooth wheel discs, O'Connor's Z did 164.461 mph to take the Class F Production Car world record.

Interesting as they are, these demonstrations of out-and-out speed were less impressive than other illustrations of the Datsun's worthiness. Albrecht Goertz, who started the Z idea, thinks that the early racing programme in America was good for the car's image, but the thing that really convinced the general public that this was a serious, durable car was winning the Safari Rally. And even at the time of the car's introduction that was a major objective, as we shall see in the next chapter.

CHAPTER 11

Objective — Safari

The rally cars

The main thrust of the factory's competition effort was in rallying. It was part of Nissan's marketing philosophy that they should demonstrate the toughness and reliability of their products in the world's classic rallies. Whether the Z would be sold in the countries where those events took place was unimportant; the kudos from success in the Safari or the Monte Carlo Rally would extend to Datsun cars worldwide.

Nissan first entered the East African Safari with Bluebirds and Cedrics in 1963. Unsuccessful at first, they persevered and, by 1969, 1600 SSS (510) saloons finished third, fifth, seventh and eighth and won the team prize. A year later, the same model had scored their first win in this toughest of rallies.

This was the time of a major European onslaught in East Africa. In Europe, rally cars were becoming more specialized and more powerful — the Mini era was giving way to Porsches, Alpines and 'homologation specials' like the Ford Escort Twin Cam. The European teams lacked the specialized engineering and the local knowledge of the Safari that Datsun had learned over the years, but it was clear that in future, even for this event, they would need a more powerful car. The six-cylinder 240Z was appearing at just the right time.

The Z wasn't — couldn't be — ready for an attempt on the Safari by Easter 1970, only four months after its announcement, but while its saloon predecessor was scoring the company's greatest motor sport success to date, the two-seater was being readied for the 1971 event. A couple of months earlier, serious testing had started in Europe. A week after the Monte Carlo Rally, when the competing teams and the world's Press had departed, a 240Z covered the entire route as part of a programme to develop a competitive contender for the following year's Monte. The driver was 1967 Monte winner Rauno Aaltonen. It was a good choice, for apart from being one of the world's top rally drivers, Aaltonen was renowned as a rally engineer with a more scientific approach to the business than most. He had driven a 1600 SSS in Datsun's first serious attempt at the RAC Rally the year before.

Britain's Tony Fall was also involved. He had met the Nissan competitions people on the 1969 Safari when driving for Lancia and appeared in a film the Japanese made about the event. The following January, Rauno Aaltonen approached him just before the Monte and said that Datsun had a new rally car in France and would he help test it afterwards? Fall — who was later to become chief of Opel's Competitions Department — vividly remembers his first encounter with the Z-car. Somewhat the worse for wear after retiring from the rally and celebrating co-driver Mike Wood's birthday, he answered a knock on the door of his hotel room at 5.30 am. A very polite Japanese asked Fall to come with him to Nice. 'We went to this grotty little garage in the back streets and they pulled the dust sheets off the car. I was horror-struck. It looked just like a streamlined Healey!' To Fall, who had forsaken BMC's ageing rally cars for more modern machinery, it did not seem very promising. But he was freelance and they were offering a very good fee, so he agreed to test it.

While Aaltonen did the full rally route, Fall concentrated on the tests of the Mountain Circuit, the *Cols* of the *Alpes Maritimes* behind Monte Carlo. He remembers: 'That first car was a disaster. It was so heavy and it bounced all over the place. I had a Japanese co-driver with me and when we came to the final test, on

Spectators' favourite — this super photograph by *Autocar's* Peter Cramer captures the fury of a rally Z in full noise. The event is the 1971 Scottish Rally and the driver is Tony Fall. He was among the leaders before the gearbox failed.

Tony Fall and Geraint Phillips were the first to take a 240Z on a rally of any kind and they chose a club event in the West of England as a try-out before this 1970 RAC Rally, from which they retired.

racing tyres, I slid wide on a corner. There was a big bang, but it bounced back on to the road and I carried on to the end of the stage. When I got to the end I realized that my companion wasn't sitting where he had been. The floor had been pushed up and his seat was right up *here,* jamming his helmet to the roof. After that I presumed that I had dirtied my ticket by shunting the car and that this would be the end of it. But in September they asked me to drive in the RAC.'

The 1970 RAC Rally was to be the 240Z's international debut, but Fall gave it an unlikely rallying baptism before that in the Torbay Rally, a minor club event in the West of England.

By then, the Z rally programme for 1971 was being finalized by Yasuharu Namba, chief of the competitions activity in Nissan's Vehicle Test Department. The rough tracks of the RAC formed a try-out for the high-set Safari-specification cars, while a separate group of Zs were being prepared by a different team of mechanics for Monte Carlo. Aaltonen's initial testing had been done with a car equipped with electronic recording equipment. For rallying in the early 1970s this was a very sophisticated approach. Some 40 sensors on the car measured everything from throttle opening to suspension deflection and stored the results on an eight-track tape recorder. He then spent two weeks, day and night, trying modifications and different combinations of components on the *Col de Turini* — running the same five-minute test route every 40 minutes.

The specification was different from the Monte cars, but even so the change from the first rally prototypes to the RAC team cars was incredible. Aaltonen and Fall were both very impressed by the way the factory had absorbed their comments and improved the cars. They had two of the RAC entries; another was Safari winner Edgar Herrmann and a fourth, last-minute entry was made for 1969 British Rally Champion John Bloxham.

Swapping *murram* for snow. 1969 Datsun Safari winner Edgar Herrmann was rewarded by a drive in the first 240Z team on the RAC Rally. The conditions were not the easiest, as the car proved difficult to handle on the secret RAC rally route and the driver was more used to the tracks of East Africa.

The first 240Z rally cars, as used on the 1970 RAC, were neat and purposeful, painted plain red with a matt black non-reflective bonnet top. However, though fairly standard in appearance, many of the body panels were actually glass-fibre (allowed by the regulations at that time).

At the time this was the first Z we had examined in detail . . . we later learned that only these works rally cars had three twin-choke Mikuni-Solex carburettors and their racing-type trumpets went some way to explaining the high noise level. So did the twin megaphoned exhaust pipes.

Considering that their rough-road testing had been limited to a couple of days' testing at the Army testing ground at Bagshot, they put on a pretty good show in their first big event. Herrmann and Bloxham were a bit out of their depth, but Fall was well placed early on and Aaltonen showed that the car was as fast as the best opposition on the quicker sections. He set best time on three special stages on his way to seventh place overall. All four cars suffered differential failures through overheating; the diff. coolers that were part of the rally specification had been removed because of the cold weather!

After the RAC Rally, the writer borrowed Aaltonen's car for *Autocar*'s 'Given the Works' series of tests on factory rally and racing cars. It was my first encounter with a 240Z; the car was not yet on sale in Europe, and though there had been one at the London Motor Show a few weeks before, there had not been a chance to drive it. As a fully prepared (then Group 3) rally machine it was hardly typical of the model as a whole. Though they were happy to let us take the car away for the weekend, the Japanese were not very forthcoming with details of its specification; the car was described as 'fairly standard'. Power

output was quoted as 200 bhp (net) and we knew that a special camshaft complemented its three Mikuni-Solex carburettors. The five-speed gearbox had closer-than-standard ratios and a direct top gear. An ultra-low 4.87:1 final-drive was combined with a limited-slip differential. Magnesium-alloy wheels, 14-inch diameter with 6-inch rims, and higher-geared steering were other obvious mods, as were the lightweight body panels allowed by the regulations at that time. Doors, bonnet and tailgate were in glass-fibre and the rear and side windows were plastic.

At the time, our performance figures — 0-60 mph in 9.0 seconds, 0-100 mph in 18.8 seconds — seemed good enough, especially since the standing-start tests had to be made very gingerly because of a suspect diff. In fact, they turned out to be more or less the same as the standard 240Z tested later. But the rally car was exactly as it had finished 2,300 miles of tough rallying, so some drop from peak performance was inevitable.

The engine was tremendously noisy, highly responsive and wonderfully torquey, but on slippery corners we soon understood why the works drivers complained of excessive understeer. To get the best out of it the Z had to be 'set up' for a corner with

Inside Rauno Aaltonen's 1970 RAC car, showing glass-fibre-shelled bucket seats set high for maximum visibility in the forests, a lot of extra switches and judiciously placed padding, and an Aaltonen trademark — tape on the steering wheel rim to indicate the straight-ahead position.

Aaltonen (right) and co-driver Paul Easter wait for differential repairs during the RAC, in which they eventually finished seventh. Note the twin spare wheels accommodated in the rear compartment with maps and other gear — the car was rather short of stowage space in the front.

Aaltonen working hard on the Monte in 1971, the car's first appearance in the European classic, which resulted in fifth place overall.

oversteer provoked by a combination of brakes and throttle; Aaltonen used the handbrake as part of that technique. The Z rally car required pretty rough treatment for the best results. That must be seen in the context of 1970. The racing-type precision of the mid-engined Lancia Stratos and the surefootness of the four-wheel-drive Audi Quattro were some way in the future.

We noted a feeling of solidity — the car seemed very stiff, even by the standards of the day — and we expressed admiration for those who could hurl what seemed a big lump of car through forests at stage-winning speeds.

They never achieved a top placing in Britain's 'Rally of the Forests', though Tony Fall ran as high as third in 1972 before the seemingly inevitable differential trouble.

The same 'sub-team' within the Vehicle Test Department, run by engineer Takashi Wakabayashi, had more success in the event that most mattered to them. They were well prepared for the 1971 Safari with 240Zs for the previous year's winner, Edgar Herrmann, a German-born hotelier from Malindi, Kenya; Shekhar Mehta, a Ugandan-Asian farmer; and Rauno Aaltonen. The Finn had a drive-shaft break and then the rear suspension collapsed; he got to the finish with winches holding the differential sub-frame in place. But after Bjorn Waldegaard's Porsche had tangled with team-mate Zasada, and Mikkola's Escort had blown a head gasket, Herrmann and Mehta found themselves running first and second. One might think that team tactics would prevail to ensure that it finished that way, but in a

scene that was to be repeated in the 1981 event, Datsun team-mates fought it out between them. Herrmann went off the road on the last leg of the rally, but stayed ahead of Mehta through the thick mud of that last section to score his second Safari win in a row. Datsun also won the team prize. It was a remarkable achievement for a car in its first full season of competition on one of the longest and fastest Safaris.

The Safari cars had slightly less power than those used in Europe, were quite a lot heavier and were even stiffer in their damping. The drivers reported that the vibration over bad surfaces was so bad that you could not focus on the instruments. The gas-filled shock absorbers used did not overcome their pistons' sliding friction over short, sharp bumps, and so under those conditions they were, in effect, solid. Datsun reckoned that very hard shock absorbers were necessary for reliability on the Safari and the results bear that out, though the compromise was not a comfortable one for their crews.

In 1972, they had two top-line drivers in one car when Rauno Aaltonen and Tony Fall shared a 240Z; it was the first time, inter-continental marathons apart, that two stars had been matched

The stud-master — Rauno Aaltonen consults with his Japanese service crew as his car is refuelled during the last night's Mountain Circuit on the 1971 Monte.

The Monte Carlo Rally cars were to a very different specification from those used on the Safari or the RAC — lower, and with more streamlining (including faired-in headlamps, Jaguar E-type-style). This is Tony Fall, partnered by Mike Wood, on the St Auban stage of the 1971 Monte.

First time out on the Safari and a win for
the 240Z, but it was the second year in a
row for Edgar Herrmann and Hans
Schuller. Though the latter was
nominated co-driver he actually did much
of the driving and also used a Z for all
kinds of competition in Africa and
Europe. Safari cars were high-set, high-
geared and with less power than those for
European events. Note the
supplementary lights mounted high on
the bonnet in streamlined pods.

1972 saw the 240Z's best result on the
Monte, when Rauno Aaltonen and Jean
Todt finished third overall — a tribute to
the development since the car's first
appearance there and the testing that had
taken place two years before.

What the Monte Carlo Rally is all about — crowds of spectators, a night on the *Col de Turini,* and a rally car in a full-blooded slide on hard-packed snow. This is Tony Fall with the Z set up the way most enthusiasts like to remember it.

together. The thinking was that since both were good mechanically and both were able to handle pace notes as well as drive, concentrated two-to-three hour stints behind the wheel would keep them at the peak of performance. The theory went wrong because they had to run most of the event without a clutch, and Aaltonen did most of the driving. They finished sixth, one place behind Herrmann, and Mehta was 10th, but this was the year of the first European win and a great Safari success for Ford. The next year Datsun were back on top. There were the same three drivers in 240Zs. Aaltonen rolled while in the lead and Mehta was left only a minute ahead of Harry Kallstrom in a Datsun 1800 SSS saloon. They ended the event with the same number of penalties — a unique situation at that time — but on the basis of 'farthest cleanest', Mehta and his very battered Z took the honours. There was some justice in this, for Mehta had been docked a minute by the scrutineers for appearing with one headlamp missing near the end of the event; in fact the car finished without one front wing!

After this second win in 1973 the Z was to have one more 'official' Safari, when Harry Kallstrom and Tanzanian Zully

Remtulla finished fourth and fifth, respectively, in 260Zs in 1974. Thereafter, the team used the Violet 160J saloon and they came back to the winner's circle in 1979.

Rauno Aaltonen remembers the 240Z as 'very close to the ultimate car for the Safari at that time'. Certainly Nissan's early view that they would need a much faster car than they had had hitherto was right. Herrmann reported running at 130 mph on his way to victory in 1971 — and being overtaken by Waldegaard's Porsche. . . .

That kind of performance, if not maximum speed or the ability to traverse everything from sharp rocks to sticky mud, was also needed for the European event that they most wanted to win — the Monte. That rally had become a Porsche benefit. The 240Zs for the Monte were lower and sleeker than the Safari cars and even used faired-in headlamp covers, like an E-type Jaguar. Aaltonen felt fairly pleased to finish fifth the first time out and set some fastest times on the mountain stages. The car's traction was excellent, but the front-end didn't grip so well and the overhang at the front meant that there was a high polar moment of inertia. It added up to a car that was fast, but in no way as nimble as the little Alpine-Renault that won in 1971 and was about to become the dominant rally car of that era. In the 1972 Monte Aaltonen was third overall and the following year he was lying second as they went into the last night's Mountain Circuit, only to have a petrol pipe break and the high-pressure pump fail. Fall and Wood finished ninth in that 1973 Monte.

Though others drove them, it is fair to give Aaltonen most of the credit for the Z's performances on the Monte Carlo Rally, not least because of the amount of work he did with tyres. Aaltonen is the master of tread patterns and studding, which can be so critical on a snowy or icy Monte, and he brought this expertize to Dunlop Japan, who supplied the tyres for studding (with Finnish studs) in France.

His car on the 1973 Monte used a fuel-injected engine with a crossflow cylinder-head. This unit, also fitted to the cars of Harry Kallstrom and Chris Sclater for the November RAC Rally, was slightly over-bored to give 2,498 cc (bore and stroke, 84.8 × 73.7 mm) developing 255 bhp at 7,200 rpm. The standard-size rally engine without the new head and on triple Solex carburettors was rated at 220 bhp.

The 'European' rally team headed by Hiroshi Komuro was less experienced in the demands of its events than the Safari crew, and on several occasions the service operation was not as slick as some of their rivals'. On the 1972 Monte, for example, Aaltonen might have been able to challenge Larrousse's second-place Porsche had the service been better planned, and Fall might not have had to retire when a drive-shaft broke. Drivers sometimes complained that the team was inflexible; that those who were operating on the rally itself were unable to take much independent action, the rally plan and particularly the cars' specifications having been decided in Japan. To be fair, their lines of communication were the longest in European rallying at the time, and once the

The 1972 Scottish Rally saw Shekhar Mehta with this ex-Safari car as one of three 240Z entrants. The layout of supplementary lamps is rather odd, but they were not needed much on this mid-summer event.

Withers of Winsford had two different British-registered 240Zs, and this one, seen here passing a crashed Escort on the 1972 Scottish Rally, was a British rally regular driven by Roy Fidler and Barry Hughes.

specifications had been decided only the spare parts to match those cars were supplied to go with them. There weren't so many 240Zs around that they could rob a vital part from a spectator's car anywhere they went.

Apart from the Monte, the European programme became increasingly selective. The factory entered the Acropolis (Mehta was sixth in 1972), the TAP Rally of Portugal (Fall, fourth in 1972) and the British internationals. Tony Fall was part of the works team for the internationals, and for other events in Britain he had the use of a Japanese-registered factory car that he ran himself. It was maintained by Datsun dealers Old Woking Motors, whose premises were used as a base by the factory team at RAC Rally time. Fall won the Welsh Rally outright in 1971, did well on the Scottish until the gearbox failed, and had a huge accident on the following year's Mintex Rally, when he and Wood misjudged the turn at the end of what Fall describes as, 'the longest airfield runway in the North of England'. Other British 240Z stalwarts were Roy Fidler, who was one of several to drive the British-registered cars run by Withers of Winsford, Malcolm Harvey-Ross, who campaigned his own Z for some

time, and Kevin Videan, who finished second in the 1975 *Motoring News* road rallying championship with his Old Woking-supported car. Chris Sclater drove for Withers and later joined the works team for the RAC (his car running on Kleber tyres instead of Dunlops in deference to his Kleber-*Wheelbase* Scholarship). For 1974 he was to drive a Violet saloon for the newly-formed Datsun UK team, but used one of the RAC 260s before the new car was ready. He ran fourth in the Welsh Rally until the gearbox broke and he also used this car in rallycross.

Several of the works team drivers obtained factory cars for their own use. Shekhar Mehta did several events this way, including the Moroccan Rally, when he crashed heavily in the desert. Edgar Herrmann's co-driver Hans Schuller used a Z in Germany and raced Datsuns as well. The Portugese importers were active and purchased two cars for local drivers. In America, where European-style rallying was in its infancy, Zs finished second and third, respectively, in the 1972 and 1973 Press-on-Regardless Rally that was the first US World Rally Championship qualifier. They also won the manufacturers' championship in the SCCA Pro Rally series from 1975 to 1977. Peter Brock's BRE team included an ex-Safari car in an attempt on the Mexican Baja off-road race on one occasion, but it turned out to have insufficient ground clearance for ploughing through sand.

The Z did well in Australian rallies. Rauno Aaltonen finished second in the Southern Cross Rally in 1972 and he might have won but for a technical infringement of the rules about advertising allowed on the cars.

History will not record the Z as one of the great rally cars and aside from African events it does not have a major rally victory in its record book. The policy was to demonstrate the ruggedness and reliability of Datsun cars and to do this a class win was often as useful for publicity as a high placing overall. There was a

Entreposto, the Datsun distributors in Portugal, obtained two 240Zs for rallying, one from Britain and the other an ex-factory Monte Carlo Rally car. This one, shown on the 1973 TAP Rally, scored a victory in the 1972 Rally of Camelias national event driven by local champion Antonio Carlos de Oliveira. It was the first outright win for the Z car in Continental Europe; Fall had won the Welsh Rally the year before.

Datsun teamed Rauno Aaltonen with Tony Fall for the 1972 Safari. It should have been a tremendous combination, but they had a number of troubles, including an inoperative clutch for most of the event, and could finish no higher than sixth.

Nearing the end of its official rally career — this Datsun Dealers-sponsored 260Z was driven by Cahal Curley, from Londonderry, on the 1974 RAC Rally. By then the other factory-supported cars were Violet saloons.

feeling that finishing and sometimes minor-category wins were more important for the team than going all-out for victory. The Safari was the exception. It was the big one that Nissan really wanted to win. The Z proved that twice.

In European rallying terms, the 240Z was old-fashioned when it arrived. Not in its looks, nor indeed in its all-independent strut-type suspension, which others envied, but in the type of car it represented. The traditional sports car in rallying was almost a thing of the past. The Porsche 911 counted as a special case and what could be seen as its shortcoming as a road car — its rear-engined design — was a positive virtue for many rallies. The era of the tiny lightweight rear-engined Alpine-Renault was dawning, and the Lancia Stratos was yet to come. The more conventional competitors used big and powerful engines in small saloon bodies. They were smaller and handier; their power-to-weight ratio was better. The Z, with its long overhang and its set-back seating position, was from another age. Some people loved them for that, and the big 240Z became a spectators' favourite on British events, just as the Healey had been. The professionals regard the rallying Z with less affection. Rauno Aaltonen claims to have no interest in cars as aesthetic objects; for him, a rally car is simply a machine for a purpose. The Z was ideal for the Safari, less so for Europe. Tony Fall has a sneaking admiration for it. 'It was like a big roller skate. There was no real sophistication in the roadholding and it was very easy to spin because of the body overhang and the short wheelbase, but it was incredibly reliable and fairly quick. If you got into trouble under braking or into a corner then it took control. You really had to be a brute with that car. You had to be determined that it wasn't going to beat you.'

Twice Safari winner Shekhar Mehta has more sentimental attachments to the Z. As late as 1981, he took part in the Janner Rally in Austria in an old 240Z. It was a snow rally in January, and he finished 12th. It was the event that provided the first win for that rally car of the 1980s, the Audi Quattro.

Shekhar Mehta won his first Safari in 1973 with his 240Z in a terrible state at the finish. He celebrates at the Nairobi finish with co-driver Lofty Drews (left) after they have been declared winners following a penalty-points tie with Datsun team-mate Harry Kallstrom.

CHAPTER 12

Buying a Z-car

What to look for

The Z-car story is far from complete as the ZX continues to be developed and is still selling strongly. However, the original 240Zs, 260Zs and (in North America) 280Zs are now obsolete. Indeed, owners of these cars may already be finding problems in locating parts and technical expertize to enable them to be kept in good condition.

As we have seen, the vast majority of Zs were originally sold in North America. Substantial numbers were sold in Europe, and in Australasia, and the publicity which followed the rallying successes might have given the impression that they were everywhere — the fact is, however, that the Z never established a truly dominant sales position outside America.

If, therefore, you are intent on buying one, decide on your priorities. In many countries there may not be a very wide choice — particularly of examples which have not suffered badly from rust or general deterioration due to poor weather conditions. In these cases, you will either have to accept whatever you can find, or on the other hand, you could go shopping in North America, particularly in California, where most of the rust-free early Zs seem to be located. The problem is that although prices may be reasonable you will be faced with the problem of getting a (left-hand-drive) car back home.

This part of the book is concerned mostly with the first series of Z-cars — those built up to 1978 — as the ZX is still current, and is a developing range of models. The choice of basically different derivatives is quite limited, but it is enough to require a little analysis. Apart from the usual decisions to be made over colour, trim and extras (not forgetting the customization which might have been applied to the car) you have to decide between the body types, and the transmission.

The first Z-car was a pure two-seater, with absolutely no provision for extra passengers, even willing and nimble children, to be carried behind the front seats. This car, in a style which carried on virtually unchanged for eight years, was only ever sold as a fixed-head coupé. When the 240Z was updated to 260Z at the end of 1973 it was joined by the stretched 2+2 derivative.

Even though the relative positions of the facia panel, steering wheel and front seats were not changed (independent magazine road tests show that the dimensions of the front cockpit are the same in each case), slightly larger doors were fitted to the 2+2, and the longer floor pan allowed a pair of rear seats to be added. Unavoidably, rear seat space is restricted, especially if the front seat passengers have long legs and need to push *their* seats well back, and the backrests are rather upright, but they are perfectly adequate for children, and useful for adults on limited journeys or, with compromise from front seat occupants, over longer distances. To make room for the rear seats, space had to be stolen from the stowage area in the tail, which is several inches shorter on the 2+2 than it is on the two-seater. On the other hand, the '+2' backrest can be folded forward when not in use, in which case there is considerably more loading area than on the two-seater. The 2+2, however, is equally as practical as — say — a Ford Capri, and much more roomy than an MGB GT or other 2+2 coupes. It lacks the pure, balanced looks of the two-seater but is, for most people, a more versatile, more practical, Z-car than the two-seater. The extra seating aside, there were few important changes to the interior of the Z during its eight-year life. A good proportion of US cars have the optional air conditioning that was not offered in Britain.

It is worth repeating that all Zs can be heavy work to drive. Power steering did not come until the ZX and the pedals and even the gearchange can require a man-sized effort. A delicate lady might find this a problem, particularly if her journeys involve a lot of parking. The car's high scuttle and sides and low seating position can also make visibility difficult for anyone small in stature.

These cars have undergone a continuous programme of engine development, primarily for North America, where the emission regulations became progressively tighter during the 1970s. US-market Z-cars were given a 2.6-litre engine at the same time as it became available in the rest of the world, but for that market only a 2.8-litre engine was offered from 1975. Because the US market was so much more important (in terms of the numbers of cars sold) than any other, the rest of the world had to accept most of the basic engine changes made for the USA. This explains, therefore, why the 240Z, with the smallest engine of the series, was also the fastest car, and it explains why the engines seem to lose their edge more and more as model-year followed model-year. So if you are shopping for a Z-car you will probably find that the older examples feel more sporting, and seem to have more acceleration, even if the penalty is that a higher grade of fuel may be needed, and that there appears to be a more limited spread of torque.

The fact that the original 240Zs were faster, most sporting, the lightest and, somehow, the 'purest' of the strain is not a unique phenomenon. Many other sports cars — British, European, and American — started out in the same way, but gradually had to give best to the stultifying regulations which flooded out of North America during the 1970s.

In America, but not in Britain, there was a choice of manual transmissions, and an automatic transmission option. The four-speed manual gearbox had a direct-drive top gear and a wide spread of intermediate ratios, while the five-speed box had a direct-drive fourth gear, a geared-up fifth gear, and closer intermediate ratios. Of the two transmissions, the five-speed box is undoubtedly the more satisfying to use, and also — if used intelligently — results in more economical motoring.

There was nothing very sporting about the Z-car when fitted with the Jatco automatic transmission, for this had the usual combination of a torque converter and three widely-spaced ratios. It took the edge off performance *and* fuel economy, left the driver virtually without control of his engine, and made it difficult to drive the Z-car as a sporting machine should be driven.

Incidentally, although you should not encounter major difficulties in finding most mechanical spare parts for a Z-car, it may be valuable extra information to know where the various major components are sourced. The various models share some components with other Datsuns of the period, but the body/chassis unit, and its rear suspension system, were unique at the time, and were not subsequently shared with any other Datsun. Only with the ZX was there significant rationalization of major components with other models — notably the 810.

The big single-overhead-camshaft six-cylinder engine has a long history with Nissan. It has been used in the larger Datsun (Cedric) saloons and estates, but was also to be found in cars like the larger Skylines and Laurels. Some of these cars still retain the original Z-car engine size of 2,393 cc, long after it had been superseded for sports car use.

The transmissions were also 'family' items, and were the largest and most robust in Datsun's range. The five-speed all-synchromesh transmission was also progressively adopted by the more sporting Skylines, Laurels and Cedrics. In most cases, however, there was little shared by the Z-car's final-drive and drive-shaft layout, and those of other large Datsuns, most of which used a rigid, 'live' rear axle.

Spare parts supply, in general, is still quite straight-forward. As with many other obsolete cars, the parts which go out of stock first are the soft trim items — trim pads, seat covering, carpets and other internal fittings — along with those parts not shared with any other Datsun. The fact that the original Z bodyshell was current until the end of 1978 means that there should still be no supply crisis of major 'consumables' like glass, body panels and important suspension items, while (for reasons of commonality already mentioned above) the supply of power-train parts should not present too many permanent difficulties. In America, there are plenty of Z-car specialists, offering everything from tuning kits to retrimming services; some are covered in Chapter 9 and a glance at US enthusiast magazines will provide more useful addresses. In whatever country you are it is always advisable to get in touch with a Z-car specialist, and also become a member of a club which caters for Z owners and enthusiasts.

In Britain, not all Datsun dealers sold Zs, but any of those that did — and deal in ZXs today — should be able to undertake maintenance and repair work.

Perhaps the leading specialists are Fourways Engineering of Borough Green, Kent, who undertake Z renovation as well as engineer and market performance and suspension conversions for Zs and ZXs.

What to look for

The fact that so many Zs have been built and sold means that they are now known as rugged, enjoyable and reliable cars, but unfortunately this does not mean that they never wear out. Indeed, it is fair to say that the Japanese reputation for making long-life cars does not entirely apply in this case. Those readers who already own Z-cars will know what I mean, while those who might soon be in the market for such a car should certainly take note of what follows.

The Z-car has a monocoque (unit-construction) body-chassis unit, and after several years it can begin to look rather scruffy and suffer from rust and general deterioration. As it is much more difficult to turn a poor monocoque into a good one than it is to restore the condition of separate bodyshell, the following points on the 1970-8 cars should be watched:

The main rust spots appear at the front of the shell. Look for evidence of rust on top of the front wings above the wheelarches, in front of the base of the windscreen pillars and down the front wings just ahead of the doors. Rust may also appear at the bottom of the doors, where the inner and outer skins are crimped together, and of course the lower sills behind the front wheels also suffer. (If a car has been fitted with mud flaps this problem is often much less obvious.) Replacement sills are available, but patching such a basic structural part is a major job.

There might also be trouble at the base of the rear wings (another splash area), on the tail panel near the taillamps and at the joints between the bolt-on front wings and the headlamp pods, not to mention the lower front panel joints under the front bumper. The most important corrosion points under the car, which could result in structural failure, are the front 'chassis' legs in the engine bay, and the main longitudinal members under the seats. These last two problem areas, on badly neglected cars, may

be almost impossible to rectify without a great deal of time, money and effort being involved. So it is worth a thorough examination underneath — on a ramp if possible.

Unless the car has been shunted and hastily repaired, it should not leak water, not even around the hatchback aperture. But if there is noise and some water entry around the door frames, this can be rectified by resetting the frames themselves.

When the cars were new, paint quality was good, so look with suspicion on any car which carries evidence of badly paint-matched panels or sections. At the time of writing, most skin panels are still available from major Datsun stockists in countries where the Z was actively marketed, along with all the glass — screen, doors, quarter and hatchback windows — and much of the soft trim. Soft trim may be needed on many older Z-cars by now, as it became scruffy quite easily. In particular, hard-used seats seemed to suffer from the splitting of welded plastic panels where the stress was highest.

In America, a number of specialists offer low-priced (by comparison) glass-fibre body panels in standard or customized shapes to replace corroded sections.

Mechanically, the story relating to older models is more encouraging. The engines, in particular, seem to go on for ever if they are properly and regularly maintained. Remember, however, that it is a big, lazy, simple engine by nature, and is rather highly tuned in Z-car form. This means that you should try to keep its oil clean, its settings to specification, and its valve gear in order. The evidence of the works rally cars and the racing Zs shows that the engine's basic strength was never in doubt.

On older cars, beware of low oil pressure (but be sure that this *is* low pressure, not a faulty pressure sensor in the block) for this may be caused by sludging or contamination of the oil ways, and one inevitable consequence is that there will be wear of the camshaft lobes and finger tappets, and an increasing loss of performance. 'Natural' camshaft wear has been regularly reported after 70,000 miles. Blown cylinder gaskets are not unknown, which in themselves are not serious, but the fact that many Zs have incorrectly set timing after the rebuild may be much more aggravating. The timing chain itself and the adjuster mechanism also wears and stretches, which does not help. It is always wise to insist on ignition and valve gear timing checks on any Z which doesn't seem to be as fast as it ought to be. Maladjusted timing

The top of the front wings and the area around the repeater indicators are particularly vulnerable to rust. This wing has been removed and partially patched; compare with the new one behind. It would be difficult to make a neat, long-lasting join at the headlamp cowl with the old wing.

not only leads to poor performance and high-speed misfiring, but also to heavy fuel consumption, which in these days of high petrol costs is not to be ignored. Oil consumption, incidentally, should never be more than 300 to 400 miles per pint. Watch for tell-tale blue exhaust smoke as an indicator of valve stem oil seal wear.

Carburettor tuning and balancing can prove tricky, and with 1973-on US cars, adapted to comply with emissions control regulations, it wasn't easy to get a carburation compromise. A solution that some American owners have adopted is to fit the carburettor set-up from an earlier model, but theoretically that's illegal.

The three types of transmission are all strong enough for the job, but none is particularly precise and sporting once wear has set in. The manual transmission boxes tended to develop sloppiness in their change on early cars, and this was mainly due to the way the gearlever was attached to the gearbox tunnel itself. To improve the rigidity of the drive-line, and thus reduce harshness and improve the gearchange, in 1972 a different type of propellor-shaft and a revised gearchange mechanism were provided. That is the Good News. The Bad News is that it is not really practical to update an original-specification car as too many components were changed.

If the car has been driven hard, eventually the gearbox synchromesh will begin to disappear, and the change itself will begin to feel notchy. Synchromesh tends to wear out first on first and second gears. The automatic transmissions seem to be good and reliable. Do not be disturbed, incidentally, if the final-drive sounds somewhat noisy and rather 'clonky', as many of the cars were like this when new, but if the backlash is excessive this may mean trouble, either in the differential itself, or in the drive-shafts. New diffs are costly, but changing drive-shafts is simpler and less of a financial problem. Their universal joints have a record of failure between 75,000 and 100,000 miles.

The other half of performance is braking, and on some of the earlier Zs the brakes were not very good. They not only suffered from fade when used hard, but tended to wear out quite quickly as well (10,000 miles is an average life for front disc pads). Wet-weather braking was particularly criticized on the first US Zs and said to be made worse by the wider wheels with which so many were fitted. The solution (long since applied to most such cars, one would hope) is to fit harder brake pads. As the car became heavier over the years British owners began to complain of fade. Brake manufacturers produced harder pads to meet this demand — Ferodo FDB76M was one such. Racing material can also be used and Ferodo offer the same pad with their famous DS11 mix. Caution: racing pads should be properly 'bedded in', can cause greater disc wear, and work properly only when warm; the apparent lack of stopping when braking gently after a cold start can be disconcerting!

A few brake servo leaks have been reported and where a replacement is necessary on a 240 it is better to fit the larger servo specified for the 260Z 2 + 2. This isn't a difficult job in itself, but finding the correct component might be.

A small point about the handbrake. Its cable is held away from the drive-shaft by a small spring that can break in time. The result is that the cable gets worn away, generating a curious and elusive noise.

Something to look out for, either when buying or as you

Headlamp housings are a separate panel, which can corrode quite badly, though they do not play any structural role. An old housing and light unit, right, with a new replacement.

continue to use a Z, is the condition of the rack-and-pinion steering mountings. In the quest for refinement these were softened as the years went on, but in any case the bushes wear and allow the rack more movement relative to the structure, which destroys the precision of the steering. The solution is to ensure that the bushes are in good condition and to shim them up or fit mountings of special material. One apparently successful North American tweak also alters the position of the rack itself, which changes the bump-steer characteristics. The use of unduly wide wheels has been known to cause excessive wear in the steering mechanism.

Another general comment is that some suspension mounting bushes seem to wear quite quickly, at both front and rear. Since this wear, if unrectified, can affect the geometry of the suspension movements, and therefore lead to irregular (and heavier) tyre wear, it is something of which any owner should be aware. Most cars of this age will by now have had one or more sets of replacement shock absorbers; their condition can have a marked effect on the Z's handling. A number of uprated shock absorber types are available (see Chapter 9) as well as the standard replacement items.

The Z is not too difficult for the home mechanic — the mechanical layout is straight-forward and there is plenty of space in the engine bay and around major components. As with any other 'classic' or 'thoroughbred' car, it pay to lavish rather more attention, and to make more regular checks, than one would do with a more ordinary saloon. A Z-car is not built like a VW Beetle and has to be treated accordingly. You would not expect a 125-mph sports car to grow old without needing some attention, surely?

Earlier in this chapter, it was recommended to contact a specialist club which looks after the needs of Zs and their owners. Such is the appeal of the car that organizations are growing up in many countries. In the United States, where most of the Z-cars have been sold when new, there are a number of clubs, organized on a regional basis. In Britain you should contact: Margaret Bukowski, Membership Secretary, Z Club, 15 Curzon Road, Ealing, London W4. Tel: 01-998 9616.

APPENDIX A
Technical specifications

Although there have been only three basic Z-cars since 1969, plus 2+2 variants of both, a number of important changes to specification have been made and these have not been the same for all markets. The table on the following pages summarizes the major variables — the engine sizes, carburation, compression ratio and power and torque figures; final-drive ratio; tyre size; dimensions and weight. Detailed on this page are the items that did not change through the Z's life and those which are common to all ZX variants. These figures are based on information supplied by the manufacturers and their importers.

Z (S30 series)

Engine: Six-cylinder in-line; cast-iron block, aluminium-alloy cylinder-head. Seven main bearings. Single overhead camshaft, chain-driven.
Transmission: Four- or five-speed all-synchromesh gearbox (ratios varied with market and model — see text). Hypoid-bevel final-drive. Single-dry-plate clutch with diaphragm spring. Optional three-speed Jatco automatic transmission with torque converter (not available in Europe).
Body/chassis: Steel, integral body/chassis with suspension sub-frames.
Suspension: Front, independent, MacPherson struts, lower links, coil springs, telescopic dampers and anti-roll bar. Rear, independent, MacPherson struts, lower wishbones, coil springs, telescopic dampers (post-1974, anti-roll bar).
Steering: Rack-and-pinion, 2.7 turns from lock to lock. 15-inch diameter wheel.
Brakes: 10.7-inch diameter disc front, 9-inch diameter finned drums rear. Vacuum servo.
Wheels: Pressed-steel disc, four-stud fixing. 14-inch diameter, 4.5-inch wide (later 5-inch steel and post-1977 British market 260Z, 6.5-inch light-alloy wheels).

280 ZX (S130 series)

Engine: Six-cylinder in-line; cast-iron block, aluminium-alloy cylinder-head. Seven main bearings. Single overhead camshaft, chain-driven.
Transmission: Five-speed all-synchromesh gearbox. Hypoid-bevel final-drive. Single-dry-plate clutch with diaphragm spring. Optional three-speed Jatco automatic transmission with torque converter.
Body/chassis: Steel, integral body/chassis with suspension sub-frames.
Suspension: Front, independent, MacPherson struts, lower links, coil springs, telescopic dampers and anti-roll bar. Rear, independent, semi-trailing arms, coil springs, telescopic shock absorbers and anti-roll bar.
Steering: Recirculating-ball type, hydraulic power assistance. 3.0 turns from lock to lock. 15-inch diameter wheel. (Non-assisted steering — not available in Britain — rack-and-pinion type; power-assisted rack-and-pinion steering on ZX Turbo in US 1981).
Brakes: Ventilated disc, 9.92-inch diameter front; solid disc, 10.59-inch diameter rear. Vacuum servo.
Wheels: Aluminium alloy 14-inch diameter, 6-inch wide (diameter, rim width and design vary with market and specification; Japanese home-market Fairlady Z has steel wheels as standard). British-market cars from 1981 standard with Dunlop Denovo 2 wheels and tyres.

300ZX (Z31 series)

Engine: V6 60-deg; cast-iron block, aluminium-alloy cylinder-heads. Four main bearings. Overhead camshafts, cog belt-driven. Hydraulic tappets.
Transmission: Five-speed all-synchromesh gearbox. Hypoid-bevel final-drive. Single-dry-plate clutch with diaphragm spring. Optional four-speed automatic transmission.
Body/chassis: Steel, integral body/chassis.
Suspension: Front, independent, MacPherson struts, lower links, coil springs, telescopic dampers and anti-roll bar. Rear, independent, semi-trailing arms, coil springs, telescopic shock absorbers and anti-roll bar.
Steering: Rack-and-pinion type, hydraulic power assistance, variable ratio. 2.8 turns from lock to lock. 15-inch diameter wheel.
Brakes: Ventilated disc, 11.8-inch front (10.8-inch non-Turbo); plain discs, 12.1-inch rear (11.4-inch non-Turbo). Vacuum servo. ABS electronic anti-lock braking available as an option.
Wheels: Aluminium alloy 16-inch diameter, 7-inch wide (Turbo), 15-inch diameter, 6½-inch wide (non-Turbo). Tyre size and type vary with market. Japanese SF specification has 5½-inch wide steel rims.

Model	Type	When produced	Where sold	Engine capacity	Bore/ stroke	Carbs/ injection	Comp. ratio
240Z 2-str	HS30/ HLS30	1970-1973 1972-1973	All export; Japan from 1972	2,393 cc	83.0/73.7 mm	2 × SU	9.0:1
Fairlady Z	S30	1969-1978	Japan	1,998 cc	78.0/69.7 mm	2 × SU	9.5:1
Fairlady Z432	PS30	1969-1973	Japan	1,989 cc	82.0/62.8 mm	3 × Solex	9.5:1
260Z 2-str	RS30	1973-1978	Europe	2,565 cc	83.0/79.0 mm	2 × SU	8.3:1
260Z 2-str	GLS30	1973-1975	USA	2,565 cc	83.0/79.0 mm	2 × SU	8.8:1
260Z 2+2	GRS30	1973-1978	Europe	2,565 cc	83.0/79.0 mm	2 × SU	8.3:1
Fairlady Z 2/2	GS30	1974-1978	Japan	1,998 cc	78.0/69.7 mm	2 × SU	8.6:1
280Z 2-str	GLS30	1975-1978	USA	2,753 cc	86.0/79.0 mm	Bosch EFI	8.3:1
280ZX 2-str	HS130	1978-1983	Europe	2,753 cc	86.0/79.0 mm	Bosch EFI	8.3:1
280ZX 2+2	HGS130	1978-1983	Europe	2,753 cc	86.0/79.0 mm	Bosch EFI	8.3:1
280ZX 2-str	HLS130	1978-1981	USA	2,753 cc	86.0/79.0 mm	Bosch EFI	8.3:1
		1981-1983					8.8:1

Max power	Max torque	Final-drive ratio	Tyre size	Wheelbase	Length	Width	Unladen weight
151 bhp @ 5,600 rpm (SAE gross)	146 lb ft @ 4,400 rpm (SAE gross)	3.9:1 (5-spd) 3.36:1 (4-spd)	175—14	90.7 in	162.8 in	64.1 in	2,300 lb
130 bhp @ 6,000 rpm (SAE gross)	126 lb ft @ 4,400 rpm (SAE gross)	3.9:1 (5-spd) 3.7:1 (4-spd)	6.45 H14	90.7 in	162.0 in	64.1 in	2,200 lb
160 bhp @ 7,000 rpm (SAE gross)	130 lb ft @ 5,600 rpm (SAE gross)	4.4:1 (5-spd)	6.95 H14	90.7 in	162.0 in	64.1 in	2,300 lb
162 bhp @ 5,600 rpm (SAE gross)	152 lb ft @ 4,400 rpm (SAE gross)	3.7:1 (5-spd) 3.36:1 (4-spd)	195/70—14	90.7 in	162.8 in	64.1 in	2,425 lb
139 bhp @ 5,200 rpm (SAE nett)	137 lb ft @ 4,400 rpm (SAE nett)	3.36:1 (4-spd)	175—14	90.7 in	169.0 in	64.1 in	2,580 lb
150 bhp @ 5,400 rpm (DIN nett)	158 lb ft @ 4,400 rpm (DIN nett)	3.7:1 (5-spd)	195/70—14	102.6 in	175.0 in	65.5 in	2,630 lb
125 bhp @ 6,000 rpm (SAE nett)	123 lb ft @ 4,400 rpm (SAE nett)	3.7:1 (5-spd)	6.45 H14	102.6 in	175.0 in	65.0 in	2,480 lb
149 bhp @ 5,600 rpm (SAE nett)	163 lb ft @ 4,400 rpm (SAE nett)	3.36:1 (4-spd)	195/70—14	90.7 in	173.2 in	64.1 in	2,800 lb
140 bhp @ 5,200 rpm (DIN nett)	149 lb ft @ 4,000 rpm (DIN nett)	3.7:1 (5-spd) 3.545:1 (auto)	195/70—14	91.3 in	170.9 in	66.5 in	2,650 lb
140 bhp @ 5,200 rpm (DIN nett)	149 lb ft @ 4,000 rpm (DIN nett)	3.7:1 (5-spd) 3.545:1 (auto)	195/70—14	99.2 in	178.7 in	66.5 in	2,850 lb
135 bhp @ 5,200 rpm (SAE nett) 145 bhp	144 lb ft @ 4,000 rpm (SAE nett) 156 lb ft	3:36:1 (5-spd) 3.7:1 (GL 5-spd) 3.545:1 (auto)	195/70—14	91.3 in	174.0 in	66.5 in	2,800 lb

Model	Type	When produced	Where sold	Engine capacity	Bore/ stroke	Carbs/ injection	Comp. ratio
280ZX 2+2	HLGS130	1978-1981	USA	2,753 cc	86.0/79.0 mm	Bosch EFI	8.3:1
		1981-1983					8.8:1
Fairlady Z	S130	1978-1983	Japan	1,998 cc	78.0/69.7 mm	Bosch EFI	8.8:1
Fairlady 280Z-L 2BY2	HGS130	1978-1983	Japan	2,753 cc	86.0/79.0 mm	Bosch EFI	8.3:1
280ZX Turbo	HLS130	1981-1983	USA	2,753 cc	86.0/79.0 mm	Bosch EFI	7.4:1
300ZX 2-str	KHLZ31	1983-on	USA	2,960 cc	87.0/83.0 mm	Bosch EFI	9.0:1
300ZX 2+2	KHLGZ31	1983-on	USA	2,960 cc	87,0/83.0 mm	Bosch EFI	9.0:1
300ZX Turbo 2+2	KHLGZ31 JTQ	1984-on	Europe	2,960 cc	87.0/83.0 mm	Bosch EFI	7.8:1
300ZX 2+2	KHLGZ31 JTQ	1984-on	Europe	2,960 cc	87.0/83.0 mm	Bosch EFI	9.5:1
Fairlady Z 2/2 Turbo	HGZZ31XT	1983-on	Japan	1,998 cc	78.0/69.7 mm	Bosch EFI	8.0:1

Max power	Max torque	Final-drive ratio	Tyre size	Wheelbase	Length	Width	Unladen weight
135bhp @ 5,200 rpm (SAE nett) 145 bhp	144 lb ft @ 4,000 rpm (SAE nett) 156 lb ft	3.36:1 (5-spd) 3.7:1 (GL 5-spd) 3.545:1 (auto)	195/70—14	99.2 in	181.9 in	66.5 in	2,990 lb
130 bhp @ 6,000 rpm (SAE nett)	123 lb ft @ 4,000 rpm (SAE nett)	4.37:1 (5-spd) 4.11:1 (auto)	175—14	91.3 in	170.9 in	66.5 in	2,850 lb
145 bhp @ 5,200 rpm (SAE nett)	166 lb ft @ 4,000 rpm (SAE nett)	3.7:1 (5-spd) 3.545:1 (auto)	195/70—14	99.2 in	178.7 in	66.5 in	3,250 lb
180 bhp @ 5,600 rpm (SAE nett)	203 lb ft @ 2,800 rpm (SAE nett)	3.545:1 (auto)	205/60—15	91.3 in	174.0 in	66.5 in	2,900 lb
160 bhp @ 5,200 rpm (SAE nett)	174 lb ft @ 4,000 rpm (SAE nett)	3.7:1	215/60—15	91.3 in	170.7 in	67.9 in	2,940 lb
160 bhp @ 5,200 rpm (SAE nett)	174 lb ft @ 4,000 rpm (SAE nett)	3.545:1	215/60—15	99.2 in	178.5 in	67.9 in	3,027 lb
228 bhp @ 5,400 rpm (PS—DIN)	242 lb ft @ 4,400 rpm	3.545:1	205/55—16(f) 225/50—16(r)	99.2 in	178.5 in	67.9 in	3,200 lb
170 bhp @ 5,600 rpm	175 lb ft @ 4,400 rpm	3.7:1	210/60—390	99.2 in	178.5 in	67.9 in	3,055 lb
170 bhp @ 6,000 rpm (JIS)	159 lb ft	4.1:1	195/70—14	99.2 in	178.5 in	66.5 in	2,755 lb

APPENDIX B

Z-car production and sales

The Z-car production lines at Nissan's Hiratsuka plant have a capacity of 11,000 cars a month — the largest sports car production in the world. In practice, the normal rate of build is between 6,500 and 7,500 per month. A total of 542,208 240, 260 and 280Zs were made between 1969 and 1978.

Throughout the Z's life, the United States of America has been its biggest market, with Japan second. Canada and Australia have vied to be a distant third to these two big sales areas, while in Europe, Great Britain is consistently the biggest market for the Z, with West Germany following closely since the advent of the ZX.

Production by model 1969-1983

Fairlady Z (2-litre)	75,216
Fairlady Z432	419
240Z	156,076
260Z (incl. 2+2)	80,369
280Z (incl. 2+2)	230,128
280ZX	382,927
Fairlady Z, ZT, ZL	31,701

Sales in the USA (figures supplied by Nissan Motor Corporation)

1970	9,977	240Z
1971	26,733	240Z
1972	46,537	240Z
1973	52,556	240Z
1974	45,160	260Z
1975	50,213	260Z/280Z
1976	54,838	280Z
1977	69,516	280Z
1978	64,459	280Z/280ZX
1979	71,983	280ZX
1980	71,533	280ZX
1981	62,800	280ZX
1982	57,260	280ZX
1983	71,144	280ZX/300ZX
1984	73,101	300ZX

Sales in Britain (figures supplied by Datsun UK Ltd)

1971	72	240Z
1972	602	240Z
1973	774	240Z
1974	588	240Z/260Z
1975	309	260Z
1976	399	260Z(2+2)
1977	418	260Z
1978	957	260Z
1979	1,205	260Z/280ZX
1980	774	280ZX
1981	785	280ZX
1982	644	280ZX
1983	500	280ZX
1984	650	280ZX/300ZX

Models sold in Britain 1971-1984

240Z	1,609
260Z two-seater	899
260Z 2+2	1,746
280ZX two seater & 2+2	3,904
300ZX	302
300ZX Turbo	217
Total 1971-1984	8,677

APPENDIX C

How fast? How economical?

You cannot always believe what you read about the performance of cars. Manufacturers' figures, particularly in years gone by, have too often related to the best run of a less than fully equipped prototype than to the car as bought by the customer. The Z's makers, Nissan, have not been notably guilty of this, but the most reliable indication of the true performance of any car is usually the independent tests of the more authoritative motoring magazines. The figures presented here are all from sources known to have the highest testing standards. They cover all the major variants of the Z from the first 240Zs to the 1984 300ZX Turbo.

As we have seen in the text, more power did not necessarily mean more performance for the Z, partly because the model put on a lot of weight, but also as a result of ever-tightening US exhaust emission-control regulations. These, and differences in specifications (see Appendix A), mean that British and US market Z cars have never had exactly parallel performance. There were also local differences for other markets, such as Australia. Japanese home-market cars in most cases had smaller engines and less power, but where specifications are similar to US models (and emissions regulations made this so in later years) performance can be expected to be similar.

Model	240Z 2-str	240Z 2-str	260Z 2+2	260Z 2-str	280Z 2-str	280ZX 2-str	280ZX 2+2	280ZX 2-str	280ZX Turbo	300ZX Turbo 2+2
Type	UK 5-spd	US 4-spd	UK 5-spd	UK 5-spd	US 4-spd	UK 5-spd	UK auto	US 5-spd	US auto	UK 5-spd
Source/ date	Autocar May 1971	Car and Driver June 1970	Autocar Aug 1974	Motor May 1974	Car and Driver June 1975	Autocar March 1980	Autocar Oct 1979	Road & Track Nov 1978	Road & Track May 1981	Autocar August 1984
Maximum speed (mph)	125	109	120	127	117	112	111	121	129	137
Acceleration (sec)										
0-30 mph	3.0	2.5	3.5	3.0	3.1	2.9	4.1	3.1	2.5	2.6
0-40 mph	4.6	3.8	5.2	4.5	4.7	4.9	5.8	4.6	4.0	4.1
0 50 mph	6.0	5.7	7.3	6 6	6.3	6.8	8.2	6.8	5.5	5.5
0-60 mph	8.0	7.8	9.9	8.8	8.3	9.8	11.3	9.2	7.4	7.2
0-70 mph	11.4	10.6	13.5	12.0	11.2	13.3	15.2	12.5	9.7	9.7
0-80 mph	14.8	13.8	17.6	15.1	15.6	17.6	20.9	16.3	12.6	12.3
0-90 mph	19.2	17.8	23.4	19.6	25.5	24.6	28.5	21.5	17.0	15.6
0-100 mph	25.6	22.8	31.1	27.5	47.5	33.7	39.9	28.5	22.0	19.9
Standing ¼-mile (sec)	15.8	16.1	17.3	16.8	16.7	17.1	18.3	17.2	15.6	15.4
Overall fuel consumption (Imp mpg)	21.4	—	23.9	22.9	—	16.7	18.4	—	—	21.5
Typical fuel consumption (Imp mpg)	24	24	25	24	24	19	20	26	24	24

The author at work — and play — on the Spa-Francorchamps circuit in Belgium.